THE
Pilgrim's
Progress

THE

PILGRIM'S
PROGRESS

BY JOHN BUNYAN

Edited and Mildly Modernized by
Hal M. Helms

With illustrations by J. D. Watson
Engraved on Wood by the Brothers Dalziel
From an 1861 Edition

PARACLETE PRESS
ORLEANS, MASSACHUSETTS

7th printing, May 1995

From the Author's Apology

And now, before I do put up my pen,
I'll show the profit of my book, and then
Commit both thee and it unto that Hand
That pulls the strong down, and makes weak ones stand.

This book it chalketh out before thine eyes
The man who seeks the everlasting prize.
It shows you whence he came, whither he goes;
What he leaves undone, also what he does;
It shows you how he runs and runs
Till he unto the gate of glory comes.

It shows, too, who set out for life amain,
As if the lasting crown they would obtain;
Here also you may see the reason why
They lose their labor, and like fools do die.

This book will make a traveler of thee,
If by its counsels thou wilt ruled be:
It will direct thee to the Holy Land,
If thou wilt its directions understand:
Yea, it will make the slothful active be;
The blind also delightful things to see.

Wouldst thou read thyself? Oh, then come hither,
And lay my book, thy head and heart together.

—John Bunyan

A Personal Word
from the Editor

One of the first books added to my fledgling "ministerial library" was a copy of *The Pilgrim's Progress.* It still holds an honored place among the books I would not want to be without.

I had first become acquainted with it through a slide presentation two or three years after my conversion. It made an indelible impression on me, as it has on millions of others through the centuries.

Written in the seventeenth century, many of the words and expressions which were in common use in those days sound strange to our ears. Some of them have become so unused that we must keep a dictionary handy in order to get the real point of what the author is saying. I found as I worked with this book, the dictionary had always to be very close indeed, and it did not seem presumptuous to think that other readers might have the same difficulty.

There was another feature of Bunyan's original work which always gave me a little difficulty. That was the style which on the page looked more like a play than a story. In the present edition I have used the more familiar narrative form.

But, even so, it seemed important to keep as much of the

flavor of the seventeenth-century original as possible, because therein lies part of its perennial charm. Some of the conversation will sound stiff to modern ears, but apparently did not seem so to earlier generations. It is well that we not lose that contact with our forebears.

This edition and revision is not designed to take the place of the original. Like the King James Version of the Bible, it deserves to be preserved, read and treasured for its own unique beauty. But just as we find a modern revision or translation of the Bible helpful in throwing additional light on the Scriptures, so, I hope, this revision will serve as a means of making Bunyan's message clearer and more enjoyable to many fellow pilgrims.

The illustrations in this edition were taken from a beautifully preserved edition published in 1861 in London. A friend of mine, John Roberts, owns the book, and kindly made it available to us. It bears, in finely written script, this dedication in the front: "W. T. Back. Presented to him by his parents on his eighth birthday, October 20, 1862." We have chosen to use these beautiful engravings, both because of their intrinsic worth and because we believe they help to preserve some of the charm and beauty of the seventeenth-century story.

— *Hal M. Helms*

BUNYAN'S TOMB

Introduction

THE JAIL — BUNYAN ASLEEP

The Pilgrim's Progress occupies "an unrivalled place in the world's religious literature." For several centuries its popularity was second only to the Bible in England, and it has been called "the most characteristic expression of the Puritan religious outlook."[2]

John Bunyan was born in 1628, in an age of religious ferment and persecution. The struggle between the parliamentary forces and the English crown eventually became a civil war, with the king losing his head, and England for a brief time becoming a republic under parliament and Oliver Cromwell. Of the religious intolerance of this time, one writer says, "Laymen and clergymen renowned for learning and piety, for opposing the views of the king's court, had their ears cut off, noses slit, faces branded with red-hot irons, were publicly whipped on the naked body, every lash bringing away the flesh, and then imprisoned with such cruelties, that when released, they could neither see, hear, nor walk."

Born in the village of Elstow, about a mile from Bedford, Bunyan was the son of poor parents. Bunyan writes, "I am thine if thou be not ashamed to own me, because of my low and contemptible descent in the world." But he goes on to say, "The poor Christian has something to answer them that reproach him for his ignoble pedigree. 'True,' may that man say, 'I am taken out of the dunghill, but I fear God.' This is the highest and most noble. He hath the honor, the life, and the glory that is lasting."

Sent for a short period to school as a boy, he tells us that he learned little and soon forgot most of that. He was quickly attracted to "evil associates," the rowdy element in the school and town, and in time became a ring-leader among them. "It was my delight," he writes, "to be taken captive by the devil at his will; being filled with all unrighteousness, that from a child I had but few equals, both for cursing, lying, and blaspheming the name of God."

In 1644, when he was sixteen years old, Bunyan was mustered into the parliamentary army, where he remained until July, 1647. Although still unconverted and living a life of sinful rebellion, Bunyan was in touch with many men of strong religious convictions in Cromwell's army, and seeds were doubtless planted in his heart to bear fruit in later life.

Soon after his discharge from the army, Bunyan married a poor but godly young woman, who brought with her two books, *The Plain Man's Pathway to Heaven* and *The Practice of Piety*. Encouraged by his wife to read these books, Bunyan began to recover his reading ability, which he had almost lost. Still he persisted in his old ways until "a loose and ungodly wretch," hearing his oaths, told him that his language made her tremble, and that he was able to spoil all the youth in the town. He was stricken by this remark, and determined to reform.

About the same time, the church-bells in Elstow were being used both to announce the morning services and the afternoon football games on the Common, although Sunday sports were considered sinful. As they were being rung one Sunday afternoon, a bolt of lightning entered the belfry and killed both the ringers. Soon Bunyan began to shun the Sunday sports he had loved so much.

He and his wife were still attending the parish church, and their first two children were baptized in it, but by this time the *Book of Common Prayer* had been replaced by the *Presbyterian Directory* to guide the public worship. Bunyan became proud of his reformation, and later admitted that at this time he "was feeding God with chapters and prayers, and promises and vows, and a great many more such dainty dishes," thinking that he was now serving God, but later feeling that he had "only got into a cleaner way to hell than the rest of his neighbors."

It was while he was engaged in his trade as a tinker or brazier at Bedford that he overheard the conversation of some women who were talking of spiritual things. He was humbled and alarmed, because he did not understand what they were talking about. "Their talk was about a new birth, the work of God in

11

their hearts, also they were convinced of their miserable state by nature; they talked how God had visited their souls with his love in the Lord Jesus. They also discoursed of their own wretchedness of heart, of their unbelief, and did contemn, slight, and abhor their own righteousness, as insufficient to do them any good. And methought," he goes on, "they spake as if joy did make them speak; they spake with such pleasantness of Scripture language, and with such appearance of grace in all they said, that they were to me as if they had found a new world; as if they were people that dwelt alone, and were not to be reckoned among their neighbours. Their talk and discourse went with me; also my heart would tarry with them, for I was greatly affected with their words, both because by them I was convinced that I wanted the true tokens of a truly godly man, and also because by them I was convinced of the happy and blessed condition of him that was such a one."

Then ensued a period of great spiritual turmoil, terror, conviction of sin, struggle — even despair. Through this struggle Bunyan became completely convinced of his lostness and need of salvation through Jesus Christ. He began to attend the meeting of a small group of open-Baptists in the town of Bedford, where he was much influenced by the preaching of John Gifford, their pastor. With his counsel and help, Bunyan began to find the release of spirit and the joy of knowing his sins had been forgiven. Into this church fellowship, Bunyan was admitted after proper inquiries had been made concerning his spiritual state, and after he had received baptism by immersion. His baptism was administered in all probability, as was then usual, at midnight, to avoid the persecution which then raged against the Baptists.

But Bunyan's path was not to be a smooth and untrammeled one. He still faced many agonies, doubts, fears and questions, as we find reflected in the story of Christian, Faithful, and Hopeful as they journeyed to the Celestial City.

Two years after joining the Baptist church, at the suggestion of "some of the most able of the saints," Bunyan began to preach. His preaching was remarkably effective, because he spoke out of the fires of his own experience and the working of God within his soul. The success of his preaching caused the Anglican divines to rise up in opposition to him, as did also the Quakers, who at that time vied with the Baptists for the allegiance of the mechanics and tradesmen, many of whom did not feel spiritually at home in the state Church.

In 1655, his first wife died, leaving him with four small children. Soon afterward, he married his second wife, Elizabeth, "who proved herself to be a most devoted wife and heroic woman." Two children were born of this marriage.

In 1660, shortly after the Restoration of the monarchy under Charles II, the twenty years of freedom the separated churches had enjoyed came to an end. Bunyan was arrested for preaching. He would neither agree to stop preaching nor would he flee, and so was lodged in jail, with the exception of a few weeks' liberty in 1666, for the next twelve years! Even so his fate was not so severe as others' who were hanged for similar "crimes."

He had been in prison for about seven weeks when he was carried before Justice Keeling, who began to argue with Bunyan concerning the virtues of the *Book of Common Prayer,* asserting that "he knew it had been in use ever since the apostles' time"! Bunyan replied that prayer must be the out-pouring of the heart, and not the reading of form. At length the judge demanded to know how he pled, and whether he confessed the indictment. Not until that moment did Bunyan know that he had been indicted. He confessed that he had gone to meetings with other Christians, that they prayed together, exhorted one another, and "that we had the sweet comforting presence of the Lord for our encouragement, blessed be his name therefore! I confessed myself guilty, no otherwise." The judge entered the plea of guilty and pronounced sentence: "You must go back again to prison, and there lie for three months; and then if you do not submit to go to church to hear divine service, and leave your preaching, you must be banished the realm; and after that, if you shall be found in this realm without special licence from the king, you must stretch by the neck for it, I tell you plainly." With that the judge ordered the jailer to take him away. "I am at a point with you," Bunyan replied to the judge. "If I were out of prison today, I would preach the gospel again tomorrow, by the help of God."

It broke Bunyan's heart to see his family in such straits. His heart was especially burdened for his oldest daughter, Mary, who had been born blind. "Oh, the thoughts of the hardships I thought my poor blind one might go under, would break my heart in pieces," he wrote later.

His family was supported as much as he was able by his own work in prison, and a fellow prisoner told later of having watched Bunyan make "many hundred gross of long tag lace." But his family was forced, nonetheless, to receive charity of friends.

As the years went on, and Bunyan continued to earn the admiration and respect even of those who disagreed with his religious views, by his exemplary conduct and obvious sincerity, he was allowed to leave jail to preach at the local church, and once going as far as London. In May, 1672, he was granted a license to preach by the King, having been formally called to become pastor of the church at Bedford. In the city of Leicester, the record shows the following: "John Bunyan's licence bears date the 15th of May, 1672, to teach as a Congregational person, being of that persuasion, in the house of Josias Roughed, Bedford, or in any other place, room, or house, licensed by his Majestie's memorand. The said Bunyan showed his licence to Mr. Mayor; Mr. Overinge, Mr. Freeman, and Mr. Browne being then present; the 6th day of October, 1672.''

The years in jail had not all been spent in making "long laces." His reading had included the Bible and Foxe's *Book of Martyrs*, a very popular account of Christian martyrs with an especially anti-Catholic bent. In prison he had written *The Holy City, Grace Abounding to the Chief of Sinners* (his autobiography), *Christian Behavior,* and *The Resurrection of the Dead.* There has been some question as to whether he wrote *The Pilgrim's Progress* during this twelve-year imprisonment, or during a six-month imprisonment he suffered when persecution arose again in 1677. The first publication of *The Pilgrim's Progress* was in 1678, but the vividness of its descriptions of spiritual struggles and the recorded testimony of a fellow-prisoner would make it seem likely that it was written during his long sojourn in prison, but kept unpublished until Bunyan was convinced that people would be helped by it. In his introductory poem he makes reference to the fact that some advised, "Publish," while others thought it too frivolous to be helpful!

On becoming pastor of the Bedford congregation, Bunyan quickly earned the nickname "Bishop Bunyan" because of his pastoral zeal and his attractive preaching. For the next sixteen years, he labored tirelessly among the believers in the Bedfordshire and East Anglia area, at times preaching in London. He vigorously defended the practice of open-communion against those Strict Baptists who would admit none to the Lord's Table except those of their own persuasion.

Among his later literary works are *The Holy War, The Life and Death of Mr. Badman, A Book for Boys and Girls,* and *The Pilgrim's Progress, Second Part,* which tells the story of Christiana (Christian's wife), her children and friends, as they went on pilgrimage to the Celestial City.

In August, 1688, Bunyan was on a preaching visit to London, and was asked to ride out through a heavy rain to Reading, to help settle a quarrel between a father and his son. On returning to London, Bunyan contracted ''a fever,'' and died August 31. He is buried in Bunhill Field, the Nonconformist burial ground in London.

BEDFORD GAOL

Who would true valour see?
   Let him come hither;
One here will constant be,
   Come wind, come weather.
There's no discouragement
Shall make him once relent
His first avow'd intent
   To be a pilgrim.

Who so beset him round
   With dismal stories,
Do but themselves confound, —
   His strength the more is;
No lion can him fright,
He'll with a giant fight;
But he will have a right
   To be a pilgrim.

Hobgoblin nor foul fiend
   Can daunt his spirit;
He knew he at the end
   Shall life inherit.
Then fancies fly away,
He'll fear not what men say;
He'll labour night and day
   To be a pilgrim.

I

Fleeing the City of Destruction

As I walked through the wilderness of this world, I lighted on a certain place where there was a Den,[1] and I lay down there to sleep. As I slept, I dreamed a dream.

Behold, I saw a man clothed with rags, standing with his face looking away from his own house, a Book in his hand, and a great burden on his back.[2] As I looked, he opened the Book, and read in it, and as he read, he wept and trembled. Not being able to contain himself any longer, he began to weep, saying, "What shall I do?"[3]

In this same condition, he turned and went back to his home, trying as best he could to keep his wife and children from seeing his distress. He could not be silent long, however, because his troubles seemed to increase. At length, he began to share with his wife and children what was in his mind. "Oh, my dear wife, and you, the children I love, I am undone by this burden that lies so heavy on my back. And more than this, I am told that our city is going to be burned with fire from heaven, and that both you and myself will come to ruin unless some way can be found for us to escape. I haven't found the way yet."

CHRISTIAN READING HIS BOOK

His family was amazed and did not believe that what he said was true. They thought that some madness had seized him. Hoping that sleep would settle his mind, they hurried him off to bed. But the night was as troublesome to him as the day, and instead of sleeping, he spent the night in sighs and tears.

When the morning came, his family wanted to know how he was. "Worse and worse," he said. He began talking to them again about his burden and his fears, but they would hear none of it. Their hearts were hardening, and they hoped by such things as harsh words they could jolt this foolishness out of him. Sometimes they would make fun of him, sometimes they would chide him, sometimes neglect him. So he began to spend more time in his own room, where he would pray for them and would grieve over his own misery. At times he would walk out in the countryside; sometimes he would read, sometimes pray. Days passed.

Then I saw him walking in the fields, reading his Book, as he liked to do, and as he read, he burst out as he had done at the beginning, crying, "What shall I do to be saved?"[4]

He looked this way and that, as if he wanted to run; yet he stood still, because (as I understood) he could not tell which way to go. Then I saw a man named Evangelist, who came to him and asked, "Why are you crying?"

The man answered, "Sir, I understand by this Book in my hand that I am condemned to die, and after that to come to judgment.[5] I find that I am not willing to die and am not ready to come to judgment."[6]

Evangelist said, "Why are you not willing to die, since this life contains so many evils?"

The man answered, "Because I fear that this burden on my back will sink me lower than the grave and I will fall into the depths of hell. And, sir, if I am not fit to go to prison, I am not fit to go to judgment, and from thence to be executed; and the thought of these things make me cry."

Then said Evangelist, "If this is your condition, why do you stand still?"

"Because I do not know where to go," he answered.

Then Evangelist gave him a parchment roll on which were

written the words, "Flee from the wrath to come."[7] The man therefore read it and, looking at Evangelist very carefully, asked, "Which way must I flee?" Evangelist pointed with his

BREAKS HIS MIND TO HIS WIFE AND CHILDREN.

EVANGELIST POINTS THE WAY TO THE WICKET-GATE.

finger over a very wide space and asked, "Do you see that narrow gate yonder?"[8]

The man said, "No."

"Do you see yonder shining light?" Evangelist asked.[9]

"I *think* I do," the man replied.

Evangelist continued, "Keep that light in your eye and go directly to it. In this way you will see the gate. When you knock at the gate, you will be told what to do."

CHRISTIAN FLEES FROM DESTRUCTION.

So I saw in my dream that the man began to run. Now, he had not run far from his own door when his wife and children, perceiving that he was leaving, began to call to him to return. But the man put his fingers in his ears, and ran on, crying, "Life! life! eternal life!"

So he looked not behind him, but ran toward the middle of the plain.[10]

Notes on Chapter 1

[1]The Bedford jail, where the author was imprisoned for twelve years.

[2]*Isaiah 64:6* We have all become like one who is unclean, and all our righteous deeds are like a polluted garment. *Luke 14:33* Whoever of you does not renounce all that he has cannot be my disciple. *Psalm 38:4* For my iniquities have gone over my head; they weigh like a burden too heavy for me.

[3]*Acts 2:37* Now when they heard this, they were cut to the heart, and said. . . "Brethren, what shall we do?" *Acts 16:30* What must I do to be saved? *Hebrews 2:2,3* For if the message declared by angels was valid and every transgression or disobedience received a just retribution, how shall we escape if we neglect such a great salvation?

[4]*Acts 16:30,31 (also above)* Believe in the Lord Jesus Christ, and you will be saved, you and your household.

[5]*Hebrews 9:27* It is appointed for men to die once, and after that comes judgment.

[6]*Job 16:22* For when a few years have come, I shall go the way whence I shall not return.

[7]*Matthew 3:7* Who warned you to flee from the wrath to come?

[8]*Matthew 7:13,14* Enter by the narrow gate; for the gate is wide and the way is easy that leads to destruction, and those who enter it are many. For the gate is narrow and the way is hard, that leads to life, and those who find it are few.

[9]*Psalm 119:105* Thy word is a lamp to my feet and a light to my path. *II Peter 1:19* And we have the prophetic word made more sure. You will do well to pay attention to this as to a lamp shining in a dark place, until the day dawns and the morning star arises in your heart.

[10]*Genesis 19:17* And when they had brought them forth, they said, "Flee for your life; do not look back or stop anywhere in the valley; flee to the hills, lest you be consumed."

2

Christian and Pliable

The neighbors also came out to see the man run, and as he ran, some mocked, others threatened and some cried after him to return.

Among those who came out, two were resolved to bring him back, by force if necessary. The name of one was Obstinate, and the name of the other, Pliable.

By this time, the man had gotten a good distance ahead of them. As they pursued him, however, they shortly overtook him, and he turned to them asking, "Neighbors, why are you coming after me?"

"To persuade you to come back with us," they answered.

The man replied, "That can by no means be. You dwell in the City of Destruction, the place where I, also, was born. I see now that it is indeed the City of Destruction, and dying there, sooner or later, you will sink lower than the grave into a place that burns with fire and brimstone. So, good neighbors, be content and go along with me."

"What!" said Obstinate, "and leave our friends and comforts behind us?"

"Yes," said Christian (for that was his name), "because all

you forsake is not worthy to be compared with a little of what I am seeking to enjoy. If you would go along with me and hold it, you shall fare as I myself. For where I am going there is enough and to spare. Come then, and prove my words."[1]

"What are the things you seek, since you leave all the world behind?" asked Obstinate.

OBSTINATE TURNS BACK.

"I seek," said Christian, "an inheritance incorruptible, undefiled, and that fades not away, one that is laid up in heaven and is safe there, to be bestowed at the time appointed on those who diligently seek it. Read it so, if you will, in my Book."[2]

"Tush!" said Obstinate. "Away with your book; will you go back with us or not?"

"No, not I," said the other, "because I have put my hand to the plow."[3]

Obstinate turned to Pliable and said, "Come then, neighbor Pliable. Let us turn back and go home without him. There is a company of these crazy-headed fools who are wiser in their own eyes than seven men who can reason with them."

Pliable said, "Don't revile. If what the good Christian says is true, the things he looks for are better than ours. My heart inclines to go with my neighbor."

"What? more fools still?" snorted Obstinate. "Listen to me and go back. Who knows where such a muddle-headed fellow as this will lead you? Go back, go back and be wise!"

Christian then exclaimed, "Nay! Come with me, Pliable! There are such things to be had which I spoke of, and many more glorious ones besides. If you can't believe me, here, read it in this Book. The truth of what is written in it is all confirmed by the Blood of Him who made it."[4]

"Well, neighbor Obstinate," said Pliable, "I begin to come to a decision. I am going along with this good man. But, my good companion, do you know the way to this desired place?"

"I am directed by a man whose name is Evangelist," replied Christian, "to speed to a little narrow gate that lies before us, where we will receive instructions about the Way."

"Come then , good neighbor," answered Pliable, "let us be going."

So they both went along together.

"And I will go back to my place," shouted Obstinate over his shoulder. "I will be no companion of such misled, fanatical fellows."

I saw in my dream that when Obstinate left, Christian and Pliable went walking over the plain, talking together as they went.

"Come, neighbor Pliable, how are you doing? I am glad you were persuaded to go along with me. Had even Obstinate himself but felt what I have felt of the powers and terrors of what is yet unseen, he would not so lightly have turned his back on us!"

Pliable replied, "My good neighbor, since there are only the two of us here, tell me now further about the wonderful things where we are going."

"I can better conceive them in my mind than I can put them into words," answered his companion. "But, since you desire to know, I will read of them in my Book."[5]

"And do you think that the words of your Book are certainly true?" asked Pliable.

"Yes, verily," Christian avowed. "This Book was made by Him who cannot lie."[6]

"Well said! What wonderful things are they?"

"There is an endless kingdom to be inhabited, and ever-lasting life to be given us, that we may inhabit that kingdom forever."[7]

"Well said! and what else?"

"There are crowns of glory to be given us, and garments that will make us shine like the sun in the heavens."[8]

"This is very pleasant," continued Pliable. "And what else?"

"There shall be no more crying, nor sorrow, for He who is the Owner of the place will wipe away all tears from our eyes."[9]

"And what company shall we have there?" asked Pliable.

"There we shall be with seraphim[10] and cherubim," answered Christian, "creatures that shall dazzle your eyes to look on them. There also you will meet with thousands and ten thousands who have gone before us to that place. None of them are hurtful, but all are loving and holy; everyone is walking in the sight of God, standing in His presence forever. In a word, we shall see the elders with their golden crowns;[11] there we shall see the holy virgins with their golden harps;[12] there we shall see men who were cut in pieces by the world, burnt in flames, eaten by beasts, drowned in the seas — all for the love they bear to the Lord of that place.[13] They will all be well and clothed with immortality as with a garment."[14]

"Hearing this is enough to ravish one's heart!" exclaimed Pliable. "But are these things to be enjoyed? How shall we get to be sharers of them?"

"The Lord, the Governor of that country, has recorded all that in this Book," Christian went on. "The substance of it is this: if we are truly willing to have it, He will bestow it upon us freely."[15]

"Well, my good companion, I am glad to hear of these things. Come on, let's increase our pace!"

Christian replied sadly, "I cannot go so fast as I would because of this burden on my back."

I saw in my dream that just as they ended this talk, they came to a very miry swamp in the middle of the plain. Not noticing it, they both fell suddenly into it. It is called the Slough of Despond.[16] Here they wallowed for a time, and were grievously covered with dirt and mud. Christian, because of the burden on his back, began to sink in the mire.

Then Pliable called out, "Ah! neighbor Christian, where are you now?"

"Truly," said Christian, "I do not know."

At this Pliable became offended, and angrily said to his

fellow, "Is this the happiness you told me of all this while? If we have such ill speed at the beginning of our journey, what can we expect between this and our journey's end? If I get out of this mire alive, you shall possess the brave country alone for me."

CHRISTIAN AND PLIABLE IN THE SLOUGH OF DESPOND

And with that, he gave a desperate struggle or two, and got out of the mire on that side of the swamp nearest his own house. Away he went, and Christian saw no more of him.

Christian, then, was left to tumble in the Slough of Despond alone. Still he endeavored to struggle to that side of the Slough farthest from his own house, toward the narrow gate. Yet he could not get out of the mire because of the great burden on his back.

But I beheld in my dream that a man came to him whose name was Help, and asked him what he did there.

"Sir," said Christian, "I was told to go this way by a man called Evangelist, who directed me to yonder gate, that I might escape the wrath to come. As I was going, I fell in here."

"But why did you not look for the steps?" asked the other.

"Fear followed me so hard," said Christian, "that I fled heedlessly, and fell in."

Then said he, "Give me your hand." So he gave him his hand, and he pulled him out and set him upon sound ground and bid him go on his way.[17]

I stepped then to the one who had pulled Christian out and asked him, "Sir, since this is the route from the City of Destruction to that gate yonder, why is it that this area is not mended, so that poor travelers might go over it more safely?"

He replied, "This miry slough is such a place as cannot be mended. It is the descent where the scum and filth that attend conviction of sin continually run, and therefore it is called the Slough of Despond. For still, as the sinner is awakened by his lost condition, there arise in his soul many fears and doubts and discouraging apprehensions. All of them get together and settle in this place. This is the reason for the badness of the ground.

"It is not the pleasure of the King that this place should remain so bad," he went on.[18] "His laborers also have, by the direction of His Majesty's surveyors, been for about these sixteen hundred years employed about this patch of ground, in case it might be able to be mended. Yes, and to my knowledge," said he, "here have been swallowed up at least twenty thousand cartloads — yea, millions of wholesome instructions that have at all seasons been brought from all places of the King's dominions (and they who can tell say they are the best materials to make good ground out of the place) — in hopes that it might have been mended. But it is the Slough of Despond still, and so will be when they have done all they can.

"True," he went on, "there are, by the direction of the Lawgiver, certain good and substantial steps, placed even through the very middle of this slough. But at such times as this place spews out its filth, as it does upon any change of weather, these steps are hardly seen. And even if they are, men, through the dizziness of their heads, miss them and fall into the mire, even though the steps are there. But the ground is good when they have gotten in at the gate."[19]

Now, I saw in my dream that by this time Pliable had arrived back at his home. His neighbors came to visit him, and

PLIABLE'S RETURN TO HIS OWN HOUSE

some of them called him a wise man for coming back, while others called him a fool for endangering himself with Christian in the first place. Others mocked his cowardliness, saying, "Surely since you began to venture, I would not have been so base as to quit because of a few difficulties." So Pliable sat shamefacedly among them. But after a while he regained his confidence, and then they all began to deride poor Christian behind his back. So much for Pliable.

Notes on Chapter 2

[1]*II Corinthians 4:18* We look not to the things that are seen but to the things that are unseen; for the things that are seen are transient, but the things that are unseen are eternal.

[2]*I Peter 1:4* An inheritance which is imperishable, undefiled, and unfading, kept in heaven for you. *Hebrews 11:16* But as it is, they desire a better country, that is, a heavenly one. Therefore God is not ashamed to be called their God, for he has prepared for them a city.

[3]*Luke 9:62* Jesus said to him, "No one who puts his hand to the plow and looks back is fit for the kingdom of God."

[4]*Hebrews 9:17-21*

[5]*I Corinthians 2:9 (quoting Isaiah 64:4)* Eye hath not seen, nor ear heard, neither have entered into the heart of man, the things which God hath prepared for them that love him.

[6]*Titus 1:2* . . . God, that cannot lie.

[7]*Isaiah 65:17* For behold, I create new heavens and a new earth; and the former things shall not be remembered or come to mind. *John 10:27-29* My sheep hear my voice and I know them, and they follow me; and I give them eternal life, and they shall never perish, and no one shall snatch them out of my hand.

[8] *II Timothy 4:8* Henceforth there is laid up for me the crown of righteousness, which the Lord, the righteous judge, will award me on that Day, and not only to me, but to all who have loved his appearing.

[9]*Revelation 22:4* He will wipe away every tear from their eyes, and death shall be no more, neither shall there be mourning or pain any more, for the former things are passed away.

[10]*Isaiah 6:2* Above him stood the seraphim; each had six wings: with two he covered his face, and with two he covered his feet, and with two he flew. *I Thessalonians 4:16* For the Lord himself will descend from heaven with a cry of command, with the archangel's call, and with the sound of the trumpet of God. And the dead in Christ will rise first. *Revelation 5:11* Then I looked, and I heard around the throne and the living creatures and elders the voice of many angels, numbering myriads of myriads and thousands of thousands.

[11]*Revelation 4:4* Round the throne were twenty-four thrones, and seated on the thrones were twenty-four elders, clad in white garments, with golden crowns upon their heads.

[12]*Revelation 14:1-5*

[13]*John 12:25* He who loves his life loses it, and he who hates his life in the world will keep it for eternal life.

[14]*II Corinthians 5:2* Here indeed we groan, and long to put on our heavenly dwelling.

[15]*Isaiah 55:1* Ho, every one who thirsts, come to the waters; and he who has no money, come, buy and eat! Come, buy wine and milk without money and without price. *John 7:37* If any one thirst, let him come to me and drink.

[16]*Despond* here means discouragement, disheartenment.

[17]*Psalm 40:2* He drew me up from the desolate pit, out of the miry bog, and set my feet upon a rock, making my steps secure.

[18]*Isaiah 35:3* Strengthen the weak hands, and make firm the feeble knees. Say to those who are of a fearful heart, "Be strong, fear not! Behold your God will come with vengeance....He will come and save you."

[19]*I Samuel 12:23* Moreover as for me, far be it from me that I should sin against the Lord by ceasing to pray for you; and I will instruct you in the good and the right way.

3

A Dangerous Encounter

As Christian was walking along by himself, he spied someone afar off, coming across the field to meet him. It happened that they met just as their paths crossed one another. The gentleman's name was Mr. Worldly Wiseman, and he dwelt in the town of Carnal Policy, a very great town not far from the one from which Christian came. Christian's setting forth from the City of Destruction had been noised abroad, so that Mr. Worldly Wiseman had heard of him and his journey. Observing Christian's laborious efforts, hearing his sighs and groans and the like, he spoke to him in this manner:

"How now, good fellow! whither away after this burdened manner?"

"A burdened manner indeed, as ever I think any poor creature had," was Christian's response. "And since you ask me, 'Whither away?' I tell you, sir, I am going to that narrow gate yonder, where I have been informed I shall be enabled to get rid of my heavy burden."

"Do you have a wife and children?" asked the other.

"Yes," said Christian. "But I am so laden with this burden

that I cannot take pleasure in them as I formerly did. I think I am as though I had none.''[1]

Mr. Worldly Wiseman looked at him shrewdly, saying, ''Will you listen to me if I give you counsel?''

MR. WORLDLY WISEMAN

"If it is *good*, I will," said Christian. "For I stand in need of good counsel."

"I would advise you, then, with all speed to rid yourself of this burden. You will never be settled in your mind until then. Nor can you enjoy the blessings God has bestowed on you till then."

Christian answered, "That is what I look for, even to be rid of this heavy burden, but I cannot get it off myself, nor is there any man in our country that can take it off my shoulders. I am going this way, as I told you, in order to be rid of my burden."

"Who bid you go this way to be rid of your burden?" asked the other.

"A man who appeared to me to be a very great and honorable person. His name, as I remember, is Evangelist."

"I curse him for his counsel!" exclaimed Worldly Wiseman. "There is not a more dangerous and troublesome way in the world than that to which he has directed you! You will find it to be so if you follow his counsel! I perceive you have already met with something, for I see the dirt of the Slough of Despond is on you. But that slough is only the beginning of sorrows that accompany those who go on in that way. Hear me! for I am older and wiser that you. In this way you are on, you are likely to meet with wearisomeness, painfulness, hunger, perils, nakedness, sword, lions, dragons, darkness, and, in a word — death and what not! These things are certainly true, and have been confirmed by many testimonies. Why should a man so carelessly cast himself away by giving heed to a stranger?"

"Why sir," replied Christian, "this burden upon my back is more terrible to me than all those things you have mentioned. No! I think I do not care what I meet with in the Way if only I can also meet with deliverance from my burden."

"How did you come by the burden in the first place?" asked the other.

"By reading this Book in my hand," said Christian.

"I thought so!" retorted Worldly Wiseman. "And it has happened to you just as it has to other weak men who meddle in things too high for them. They suddenly fall into the same distractions as you have done — distractions that not only unman men, but run them upon desperate ventures, to obtain they know not what!"

"I know what I would obtain," Christian rejoined. "I would obtain ease for my heavy burden!"

"But why will you seek for ease this way, seeing that so many dangers accompany it? Especially since I could direct you to get what you desire without these dangers that you will meet if you continue in this way, if only you had patience to listen to me. Besides," Worldly Wiseman continued, "I will add that, instead of those dangers, you will meet with much safety, friendship and contentment."

"Sir," said Christian hopefully, "I pray, open this secret to me."

Worldly Wiseman proceeded: "In yonder village, Morality, there lives a gentleman whose name is Legality — a very judicious man, a man of very good reputation. He has skill to help men off with such burdens as yours. To my knowledge he has done a great deal of good in this way. Yes, and besides, he has skill to cure those who are somewhat crazed in their wits with their burdens. To him, as I said, you may go and be helped very quickly. His house is not quite a mile from here, and if he is not at home, he has a son, whose name is Civility, who can help you quite as well as the old gentleman himself. There you may be eased of your burden, and if you don't feel like going back to your former home (as indeed I would not wish you to do) you may send for your wife and children and find a home in this village at a reasonable rate. Provision there is cheap and good. What will make your own life even more happy is that in this village you are sure to be living among honest neighbors, in credit and good fashion."

Christian was confused by this speech. Presently he concluded, "If what this gentleman has said is true, my wisest course is to take his advice." With that he said, "Sir, which is the way to this honest man's house?"

"Do you see that high hill over there?"

"Yes, very well."

"By that hill you must go," said Worldly Wiseman. "And the first house you come to is his."

So Christian turned out of his way to go to Mr. Legality's house for help. But, behold, when he was very close to the hill, it seemed so high, and the side next to him seemed to hang over the road in such a dangerous way, that Christian was afraid to venture farther, lest the hill should fall on his head. So he stood still, not knowing what to do. His burden, too, seemed even heavier than before. There came also flashes of lightning out of the hill, so that Christian was afraid he would be burnt, and he began to sweat and tremble with fear.

He was sorry now that he had listened to Mr. Worldly Wiseman's counsel. While he stood there, not knowing what to do, he saw Evangelist coming towards him. At the sight of him, Christian blushed for shame. Coming up to him, Evangelist looked at him with a severe and dreadful countenance, and thus began to talk with Christian:

"What are you doing here, Christian?" said he. Christian did not know how to answer, so he stood there speechless before him. Evangelist went on, "Are you not the man that I found crying outside the City of Destruction?"

"Yes, dear sir, I am the man."

"Did not I direct you the way to the little narrow gate?"

"Yes, dear sir," said Christian.

"How is it then, that you are so quickly turned aside? For you are now out of the Way," said Evangelist.

"I met with a gentleman soon after I got over the Slough

MOUNT SINAI

of Despond," explained Christian. "He persuaded me that I might, in this village before me, find a man who could take off my burden."

"What was he?" asked Evangelist.

"He looked like a gentleman, and talked much to me, and got me at last to yield. So I came this way, but when I beheld this hill and how it hangs over the road, I stopped for fear it would fall on my head."

"What did that gentleman say to you?"

"He asked me where I was going, and I told him."

"And what did he say then?" Evangelist persisted.

"He asked me if I had a family, and I told him. 'But,' said I, 'I am so laden with the burden on my back that I cannot take pleasure in them as formerly.'"

"And what did he say then?"

Christian answered, "He bid me to get rid of my burden quickly, and I told him this is what I wanted to do. 'And,' said I, 'I am going to that wicket gate yonder to receive further direction on how I may get to the place of deliverance.' So he said that he would show me a better and shorter way, not so attended with difficulties as the Way, sir, that you sent me in. 'Which way,' said he, 'will direct you to a gentleman's house who has skill to take off these burdens.' So I believed him, and turned out of that Way into this one, hoping that I might soon be eased of my burden. But when I came to this place, and saw things as they are, I stopped for fear of danger, as I said. Now, I do not know what to do."

Then said Evangelist, "Stand still a little, so that I may show you the words of God."

He stood, trembling. Then said Evangelist, "See that you do not refuse him who is speaking; for if they did not escape when they refused him who warned them on earth, much less shall we escape if we reject him who warns from heaven."[2] And again, "The just shall live by faith; but if he draws back, my soul shall have no pleasure in him."[3] Then he applied these words thus: "You are a man who is running into misery. You have begun to reject the counsel of the Most High, and to draw back your foot from the Way of peace, even almost to the point of your utter ruin.''

Christian fell down at his feet as dead, crying, ''Woe is me, for I am undone!''

Evangelist caught him by the right hand, saying, ''All manner of sin and blasphemies shall be forgiven men.[4] Be not faithless, but believing.''[5] Christian then revived a little, and stood up again, still trembling.

Evangelist then proceeded, saying, ''Give more earnest heed to the things that I shall tell you. I will show you who has deluded you, and who it was to whom he sent you. The man who met you is one Worldly Wiseman, rightly so called, because he likes only the teaching of this world.[6] For this reason he always goes to the town of Morality to church. The reason he loves the world's doctrine best is that it saves him from the Cross.[7] Because he is of this carnal or fleshly temper, he seeks to pervert my ways, although they are right. There are three things in this man's counsel that you must utterly abhor and avoid:

First, that he turned you out of the Way.

Second, that he tried to make the Cross odious to you.

Third, that he set your feet in that way that leads to the ministration of death.

''First — you must abhor his turning you out of the Way; yes, and your own consenting to it, because this is to reject the counsel of God for the sake of the counsel of a worldly wiseman. The Lord says, 'Strive to enter in at the narrow gate,'[8] the gate to which I send you; 'for narrow is the gate which leads to life, and few there are who find it.'[9] From this little wicket gate, and from the way to it, this wicked man has turned you, bringing you almost to destruction. Hate, therefore, his turning you out of the Way and abhor yourself for listening to him.

"Secondly — you must abhor his efforts to make the Cross odious to you, because you are to prefer the Cross above all the treasures of Egypt.[10] The King of Glory has told you that he who will save his life will lose it, and that he who comes after Him, and does not hate father, mother, wife, children, brothers and sisters, yes, and his own life also, he cannot be his disciple.[11] I say, then, for a man to labor to persuade you that the very thing will be death to you without which the Truth says you cannot have eternal life, this teaching you must abhor and hate.

"Thirdly — you must hate his setting your feet in the way that leads to the ministration of death. And for this you must consider to whom he sent you and how unable that person is to deliver you from your burden.

"The one to whom you were sent is named Legality, the son of a slave who is now in bondage with her children,[12] and this mountain which you feared would fall on your head is Mount Sinai. Now if she with her children is in slavery, how can you expect to be made free by them? This Legality, therefore, is not able to free you from your burden. No man was as yet ever rid of his burden by him, nor is ever likely to be. You cannot be justified by works of the law, for by the deeds of the law no man living can be rid of his burden.[13] Therefore, Mr. Worldly Wiseman is an alien and Mr. Legality is a cheat; and as for his son, Civility, notwithstanding his simpering looks, he is but a hypocrite and cannot help you. Believe me, there is nothing in all this noise that you have heard from these foolish men, but a design to beguile you and cheat you of your salvation by turning you from the Way in which I had set you."

After this, Evangelist called aloud to the heavens for confirmation of what he had said, and with that there came words and fire out of the mountain under which poor Christian stood, which made the hair of his flesh stand up. The words were thus pronounced: "As many as are under the works of the law are under a curse: for it is written, 'Cursed is everyone who continues not in all the things which are written in the book of the law to do them.' "[14]

Now Christian looked for nothing but death, and began to cry and lament, even to curse the time when he met Mr. Worldly Wiseman. He called himself a fool a thousand times over, to think that this gentleman's arguments, flowing only from the flesh, should have won him over so far as to cause him to forsake the right way. This done, he applied himself again to Evangelist in words something like this:

"Sir, what do you think? Is there any hope? May I now go back and go up to the wicket gate? Shall I not be abandoned for this, and sent back condemned? I am sorry that I have listened to this man's counsel. May my sin be forgiven?"

"Your sin is very great," answered Evangelist, "for by it you have committed two evils: you have forsaken the Way that is good and have walked in forbidden paths. Yet will the man at the gate receive you. But take heed, that you turn not aside again, lest you perish from the way when his wrath is kindled but a little."[15]

Christian turned himself to go back, and Evangelist, when he had kissed him, gave him a smile and bid him Godspeed. So he went on with haste; neither did he speak to anyone by the way, nor if anyone asked him anything did he give an answer. He went like one who was all the time walking on forbidden ground, and who could not think himself safe till again he was back in the Way he had left to follow Mr. Worldly Wiseman's counsel. So, in the process of time, Christian got up to the gate.

Notes on Chapter 3

[1] *I Corinthians 7:29*

[2] *Hebrews 12:25*

[3] *Hebrews 10:38*

[4] *Matthew 12:31*

[5] *John 20:27*

[6] *I John 4:5* They are of the world, therefore what they say is of the world, and the world listens to them.

[7] *Galatians 6:12* It is those who want to make a good showing in the flesh that would compel you to be circumcised, and only in order that they may not be persecuted for the cross of Christ.

[8] *Luke 13:24*

[9] *Matthew 7:13,14*

[10] *Hebrews 11:25,26*

[11] *Mark 8:38; John 12:25; Matthew 10:39; Luke 14:26*

[12] *Galatians 4:21-27* Tell me, you who desire to be under law, do you not hear the law? For it is written that Abraham had two sons, one by a slave and one by a free woman. But the son of the slave was born according to the flesh, the son of the free woman through promise. Now this is an allegory: these women are two covenants. One is from Mount Sinai, bearing children for slavery; she is Hagar. Now Hagar is Mount Sinai in Arabia, she corresponds to the present Jerusalem, for she is in slavery with her children. But the Jerusalem above is free, and she is our mother. For it is written,
"Rejoice, O barren one that dost not bear;
break forth and shout, thou who art not in travail;
for the desolate hath more children than she who hath a
husband."

[13] *Galatians 3:11*

[14] *Galatians 3:10*

[15] *Psalm 2:12*

4
Christian Reaches the Wicket Gate

O ver the wicket gate there was written: "Knock, and it shall be opened unto you."[1]

He knocked, therefore, more than once or twice, saying:

> *May I now enter here? Will He within*
> *Open to sorry me, though I have been*
> *An undeserving rebel? Then shall I*
> *Not fail to sing His lasting praise on high.*

At last there came a grave person to the gate, named Goodwill, who asked who was there, where he came from, and what he would have.

Christian said, "Here is a poor burdened sinner. I come from the City of Destruction, but I am going to Mount Zion so that I may be delivered from the wrath that is to come. Since I have been told that by this gate is the way to Mount Zion, I would know, sir, if you are willing to let me in."

"I am willing with all my heart," replied Goodwill. And with that he opened the gate.

CHRISTIAN KNOCKING AT THE GATE

When Christian was stepping in, the other man gave him a quick pull.

"What does that mean?" asked Christian.

"A little distance from this gate there is a mighty castle of which Beelzebub is the captain," said Goodwill. "From there, both he and those who are with him shoot arrows at those who come up to this gate, hoping they may die before they can enter."

"I rejoice and tremble," said Christian.

When Christian was safely in, the man of the gate asked him who had directed him to the gate.

He answered, "Evangelist directed me to come here and knock, as I did. And he said that you, sir, would tell me what I must do."

"An open door is set before you, and no man can shut it," said Goodwill.

"Now I begin to reap the benefit of my dangers!" exclaimed Christian.

"But how is it that you came alone?"

"Because none of my neighbors saw their danger as I saw mine."

"Did any of them know of your coming?"

"Yes," said Christian, "my wife and children saw me at the first, and called after me to turn around. There were also some of my neighbors who cried after me to return, but I put my fingers in my ears, and so came on my way."

"But did not one of them follow you, to persuade you to go back?" asked Goodwill.

"Yes," he answered, "both Obstinate and Pliable. But when they saw that they could not prevail, Obstinate went back railing and shouting, and Pliable came with me a little way."

"But why did he not come through to the gate?"

"We both came together," said Christian, "until we came to the Slough of Despond, where we both fell. My neighbor, Pliable, was then discouraged and would adventure no farther. He got out of the slough on the side nearest to his home and told me that I should possess the brave country alone for him. He went his way and I went mine — he after Obstinate, and I to this gate.''

"Alas, poor man!'' sighed Goodwill. "Is the celestial glory of so little value that he does not count it worth the danger of a few difficulties to obtain it?''

Replied Christian, "Truly I have spoken the truth about Pliable and, if I should also say the truth about myself, it will be plain that there is not a choice between us. It's true, he went back to his own house, but I also turned aside to go into the way of death, being persuaded that way by the carnal argument of one Mr. Worldly Wiseman.''

"Oh, did he light upon you?'' exclaimed Goodwill. "He would have you seek for ease at the hands of Mr. Legality! They are both cheats. But did you take his counsel?''

"Yes, as far as I dared,'' said Christian. "I went to find Mr. Legality, until I thought that the mountain that stands by his house would fall on my head, and I was forced to stop.''

"That mountain has been the death of many and will be the death of many more.'' Goodwill shook his head. "It is well you escaped being dashed in pieces by it.''

"Truly, I do not know what would have become of me had not Evangelist happily met me again as I was musing in the midst of my dumps. But it was God's mercy that he came to me again, for else I would never have arrived here. But now, here I am, such as I am — more fit indeed for death by that mountain than to be standing talking with my Lord. But oh, what a favor is this to me that I am yet admitted entrance here!''

"We make no objections against any,'' said Goodwill, "notwithstanding all that they have done before they arrived. They in no wise are cast out.[2] Therefore, good Christian, come a little way with me, and I will teach you about the Way you must travel. Look ahead of you. Do you see this narrow Way? That is the Way you must go. It was built up by the patriarchs, prophets, Christ and His apostles, and it is as straight as a rule can make it: this is the Way you must go.''

Christian queried, ''But are there no turnings or windings, by which a stranger may lose his way?''

''Yes, there are many ways that butt down on this one, and they are crooked and wide. But this is the way you may distinguish the right from the wrong: the right only is straight and narrow.''[3]

Then I saw in my dream that Christian asked him further if he could not help him off with his burden that was on his back, for as yet he had not gotten rid of it and could not get it off by any means without help.

''As to your burden,'' said Goodwill, ''be content to bear it until you come to the place of deliverance, for there it will fall from off your back by itself.''

Then Christian began to gird up his loins and to address himself to his journey. Goodwill told him that before he had gone very far, he would come to the house of the Interpreter, at whose door he should knock, and he would show him excellent things.

Then Christian took his leave of his friend, and Goodwill again bid him Godspeed.

Notes on Chapter 4

[1] *Matthew 7:7*

[2] *John 6:37* All that the Father gives me will come to me; and him who comes to me I will not cast out.

[3] *Matthew 7:13,14*

5
At the Interpreter's House

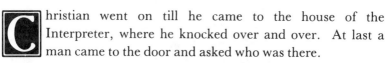hristian went on till he came to the house of the Interpreter, where he knocked over and over. At last a man came to the door and asked who was there.

"Sir, here is a traveler," Christian responded, "who was bidden by an acquaintance of the good man of this house to call here for his profit. I would, therefore, speak to the master of the house."

So he called for the master of the house, and after a little time he appeared and asked Christian what he would have.

Christian said, "Sir, I am a man who has come from the City of Destruction and am going to Mount Zion. I was told by the man who stands at the gate at the head of this road that if I called here you would show me excellent things which would be helpful to me on my journey."

"Come in," answered the Interpreter. "I will show you that which will be profitable to you."

So the master commanded his helper to light a candle and bade Christian to follow him. They went into a private room, where Christian saw the picture of a very serious-looking person hanging against the wall. It had eyes lifted up to

Heaven, the best books in its hands, the law of truth written upon its lips, and the world behind its back. It stood as if it pleaded with men, and a crown of gold hung over its head.

"What does this mean?" asked Christian.

GOD'S MINISTER

"The man whose picture this is is one of a thousand," answered the Interpreter. "He can say in the words of the apostle, 'Though you have countless guides in Christ, you do not have many fathers. For I became your father in Christ Jesus through the gospel....My little children, with whom I am again in travail until Christ be formed in you.'[1] You see that his eyes are lifted up to Heaven, that he has the best of books in his hand, and the law of truth upon his lips — this is to show you that his work is to know and unfold hidden things to sinners, just as you also see him standing as if he pleaded with men. As you can see the world as though it were cast behind him, and that a crown hangs over his head, — this is to show that slighting and despising things that are present for the love he has to his Master's service, he is sure in the world to come to have glory for his reward. Now, I have shown you this picture first because the man whose picture this is, is the only man whom the Lord of the City to which you are going has authorized to be your guide. He has been authorized to help in all difficult places you may meet with in the Way. So take good heed to what I have shown you, and keep well in mind what you have seen, lest in your journey you meet with some who pretend to lead you right, but whose way goes down to death!"

Then, taking Christian by the hand, the Interpreter led him into a very large parlor, full of dust as though it was never swept. When they had looked at it for a little while, the Interpreter called for a man to sweep. As the room was swept, the dust flew about so abundantly that Christian almost choked on it. Then said the Interpreter to a young woman who stood by, "Bring water and sprinkle the room."

When she had done this, the room was swept and cleaned with ease.

"What does this mean?" asked Christian.

The Interpreter answered: "This parlor is the heart of a

man that was never sanctified by the sweet grace of the Gospel. The dust is his original sin and the inward corruptions that have defiled the whole man. He that began to sweep at first is the Law, but she that brought water and sprinkled the room with it is the Gospel. Now you saw that as soon as the man began to sweep, the dust flew about so much that the room could not be cleansed, but, instead, you were almost choked with the dust. This is to show you that the Law, by its working, instead of cleansing the heart from sin, actually revives and puts strength into it and increases it in the soul, even as it uncovers sin and forbids it. The Law does not give power to subdue sin.[2]

"Again, you saw the young woman sprinkle the room with water, and afterward the room was easily cleansed. This is to show you that when the Gospel comes in, the sweet and precious influences of it so affect the heart, as you saw the young woman lay the dust by sprinkling the floor with water, that sin is vanquished and subdued, and the soul is made clean, through the faith of the Gospel, and consequently the soul is made fit for the King of Glory to inhabit."[3]

I saw then in my dream that the Interpreter took him by the hand and led him into a little room where there were two children, each in his chair. The name of the older was Passion, and the name of the other, Patience. Passion seemed to be very discontented, but Patience was very quiet.

Then Christian asked, "What is the reason of the unhappiness in Passion?"

"Their governess would have him wait for his best things till the beginning of next year, but he wants all of it now," replied the Interpreter. "Patience, however, is willing to wait."

Then I saw that someone came to Passion and brought him a bag of treasure and poured it down at his feet. He took it up and was very happy with it, laughing Patience to scorn. But I watched for a while, and saw that he had wasted it all away and had nothing left him but rags.

"Expound this matter more fully to me," said Christian.

"These two lads," Interpreter continued, "are figures.

PASSION AND PATIENCE

Passion is a picture of the men of this world, and Patience is one of the world which is to come. As you can see, Passion wants all now, this year — that is to say, in this world. So are the men of this world: they must have all their good things now. They cannot wait till next year — that is, until the next world, for their portion of good. That proverb, 'A bird in the hand is worth more than two in the bush,' is of more authority to them than all the divine testimonies of the world to come. But as you saw that he quickly lavished all away and soon had nothing left but rags, so will it be for all such men at the end of this world."

Christian responded, "I see that Patience has the greater wisdom on several accounts: first, because he waits for the best things, and also because he will have the glory and joy of his when the other has nothing but rags."

"You may add another," continued Interpreter. "The glory of the next world will never wear out, but that of this world is suddenly gone. Therefore Passion never had so much reason to laugh at Patience as Patience will have to laugh at Passion. First must give place to last, because last must have his time to come. But last gives place to nothing, for there is not another to succeed him. He who has his portion first surely must have time to spend it. But he who has his portion last must have it lastingly. Therefore, it is said of Dives, the rich man, 'In your lifetime you received your good things, and Lazarus in like manner evil things; but now he is comforted here, and you are in anguish.' "[4]

"I perceive, then," Christian observed, "that it is not best to covet things that are now, but to wait for things to come."

"You say truth," replied his friend. " 'For the things that are seen are temporal, but the things that are not seen are eternal.'[5] But though this is so, yet since things present and our fleshly appetites are such good neighbors to one another, and because things to come and carnal sense are such strangers to one another, that is why it is so easy to be like Passion and so hard to be like Patience."[6]

Then I saw in my dream that the Interpreter took Christian by the hand and led him into a place where there was a fire burning in a fireplace. Someone standing by it was always casting water on it to put it out. Yet, in spite of this, the fire continued to burn higher and hotter.

Again Christian asked what the scene meant.

Interpreter said, "This fire is the work of grace that is worked in the heart. He who casts water on it to extinguish it and put it out is the Devil. I will show you the reason why, in spite of his efforts to put the fire out, it burns hotter and higher."

With that, he led him around to the other side of the wall where he saw a man with a vessel of oil in his hand, from which he continually but secretly poured oil into the fire.

"This," continued the Interpreter, "is Christ, who continually, with the oil of His grace, maintains the work already begun in the heart. It is because of this that, in spite of all the Devil can do, the souls of His people prove gracious still.[7] And the fact that the man with the oil stands behind the wall to maintain the fire shows that it is hard for the tempted to see how this work of grace is maintained in the soul."

I saw also that the Interpreter took him by the hand and led him into a pleasant place where there was a stately palace, beautiful to behold. At the sight of this, Christian was greatly delighted. He saw also upon the top of the palace, certain persons walking who were clothed all in gold.

"May we go higher?" he asked.

Then the Interpreter led him up toward the door, where a great company of men were standing, desiring to go on, but dared not. There also sat a man at a little distance from the door beside a table, with a book and his inkhorn in front of him, to take the names of those who should enter the palace door. Christian also saw that in the doorway stood many men in armor to guard it, who were resolved to do whatever hurt or mischief they could to any who entered the door.

Christian was somewhat confused by this, and as he looked

he saw a man of very stout countenance come up to the man who sat by the writing table, saying, "Set my name down, sir." When that was done, the man drew his sword, put a helmet upon his head and rushed toward the door upon the armed men, who laid upon him with deadly force. But the man, not at all discouraged, began cutting and hacking most fiercely. So after receiving many wounds and giving many

THE MAN OF STOUT COUNTENANCE

wounds to those who tried to keep him out,[8] he cut his way through them all and pressed forward into the palace. This being done, there was a pleasant voice heard from those inside, even those who walked on the top of the palace, saying:

Come in, come in;
Eternal glory thou shalt win.

62

So the man went in, and there was clothed with such garments as they wore. Christian smiled and said, "I think truly I know the meaning of this."

Christian felt he was ready to resume his journey, but Interpreter said, "Stay until I have shown you a little more, and then you may go your way."

Again he led him into a very dark room, where a man sat in an iron cage.

Now the man seemed very sad, and sat with his eyes looking

THE MAN IN THE CAGE

to the ground, his hands folded together, sighing as if his heart was breaking.

The Interpreter invited Christian to talk with the man.

"What are you?" asked Christian.

"I am what I was not once," was the reply.

"What were you once?" he asked.

The man replied, "I was once a fair and flourishing professing Christian,[9] both in my own eyes and in the eyes of others. I was once, as I thought, on my way to the Celestial City, and even had joy at the thoughts that I should get there."

"Well then," said Christian again, "what are you now?"

"I am a man of despair," he answered. "I am shut up in it, as in this iron cage. I cannot get out! Oh, now I cannot!"

"But how did you get into this condition?" persisted Christian.

The man said, "I stopped watching and being sober. I gave in to my lusts. I sinned against the light of the Word and the goodness of God. I have grieved the Spirit, and He is gone. I tempted the Devil, and he came to me. I have provoked God to anger and He has left me. I have so hardened my heart that I cannot repent."

"For what did you bring yourself into this condition?" asked Christian.

"For the lusts, pleasures and profits of this world," the man answered. "In the enjoyment of these things, I promised myself much delight, but now every one of those things bites and gnaws me, like a burning worm."

Interpreter interjected, "Let this man's misery be remembered by you and be an everlasting warning to you."

"Well, this *is* fearful!" exclaimed Christian. "God help me to watch and be sober and to pray so that I may shun the cause of this man's misery."

Christian was becoming a little eager to leave, but Interpreter again bid him wait for one thing more. "Then," he said, "you may go on your way."

So he led Christian into yet another room, where there was a man rising out of bed. As he put his clothes on, he shook and trembled.

Then said Christian, "Why does this man tremble so?"

The Interpreter bid the man tell the reason for his trembling to Christian, and he spoke thus:

"This night, as I was in my sleep, I dreamed, and behold, the heavens grew exceeding black. It thundered and lightened

THE MAN'S DREAM

65

in the most fearful way, so that it put me in agony. So I looked up and saw the clouds moving at an unusual rate, and heard a great sound of a trumpet. Then I saw a Man sitting upon a cloud, attended with the thousands of Heaven. They were all in flaming fire, as were the heavens, too. Then I heard a great voice saying: 'Arise, you dead, and come to judgment.' And with that, the rocks split, the graves opened, and the dead in them came forth. Some of them were exceeding glad and looked upward, while others sought to hide themselves under the mountains. Then I saw the Man that sat upon the cloud open the Book and bid the world draw near. Yet there was, because of the flame which issued out and came before him, a considerable distance between Him and them, as between the judge and the prisoners at the bar.[10] I heard it also proclaimed to them who attended the Man who sat on the cloud, 'Gather together the tares, the chaff, and stubble, and cast them into the burning lake.'[11] And with that the bottomless pit opened, almost where I stood. Out of the mouth of it there came much smoke and coals of fire, with hideous noises. To the same attendants, it was said, 'Gather the wheat into his store-houses.'[12] And with that I saw many caught up and carried away in clouds, but I was left behind.[13] I, too, sought to hide myself, but I could not, for the Man who sat upon the cloud still kept his eye on me; my sins came to my mind and my conscience accused me on every side.[14] Just then, I awakened from my sleep.''

''But what was it that made you so afraid at this sight?'' asked Christian.

''Why, I thought the day of judgment had come,'' answered the other, ''and I thought I was not ready for it. This was what frightened me most, that the angels gathered up others and left me behind. Then, too, the pit of Hell opened her mouth just where I stood; and my conscience, too, afflicted me. I thought, too, as the Judge was keeping his eye on me, that he showed indignation in his countenance.''

The Interpreter then put a question to Christian: ''Have you considered all these things?''

''Yes,'' he replied, ''and they put me in hope and fear.''

''Then keep all these things so in your mind that they become like goads in your side, to prick you forward in the way you must go,'' said the Interpreter.

As Christian began to gird up his loins and prepare himself for his journey, Interpreter spoke again:

''The Comforter be always with you, good Christian, to guide you in the way that leads to the city.''

So Christian went on his way, saying:

> *Here have I seen things rare and profitable;*
> *Things pleasant, dreadful; things to make me stable*
> *In what I have begun to take in hand;*
> *Then let me think on them, and understand*
> *Why they were shown to me; and let me be*
> *Thankful, O good Interpreter, to thee.*

Notes on Chapter 5

[1] *I Corinthians 4:15* and *Galatians 4:19*

[2] *Romans 7:9* I was once alive apart from the law, but when the commandment came, sin revived, and I died. *I Corinthians 15:56* The sting of death is sin, and the power of sin is the law. *Romans 5:20* Law came in, to increase the trespass; but where sin increased, grace abounded all the more.

[3] *John 15:3* You are already made clean by the word which I have spoken to you. *Ephesians 5:26* ...That he might sanctify her, having cleansed her by the washing of water with the word. *Acts 15:9* And he made no distinction between us and them, having cleansed their hearts by faith. *Romans 16:25,26* Now to him who is able to strengthen you according to my gospel and the preaching of Jesus Christ, according to the revelation of the mystery which was kept secret for long ages, but is now disclosed and through the prophetic writings is made known to all nations, according to the command of the eternal God, to bring about obedience to the faith... *John 15:13* Greater love hath no man than this, that a man lay down his life for his friends.

[4] *Luke 16:25*

[5] *II Corinthians 4:18*

[6] *Romans 7:15-25*

[7]*II Corinthians 12:9* But he said to me, "My grace is sufficient for you, for my power is made perfect in weakness." I will all the more gladly boast of my weaknesses, that the power of Christ may rest upon me.

[8]*Matthew 11:12* From the days of John the Baptist until now the kingdom of heaven has suffered violence, and men of violence take it by force. *Acts 14:22* Strengthening the souls of the disciples, exhorting them to continue in the faith, saying that through many tribulations we must enter the kingdom of God.

[9]*Luke 8:13* And the ones on the rock are those who, when they hear the word, receive it with joy; but these have no root; they believe for a while, and in time of temptation, fall away.

[10]*I Corinthians 15:51-58; I Thessalonians 4:16* For the Lord himself will descend from heaven with a cry of command, with the archangel's call, and with the sound of the trumpet of God. *Jude 14,15* Behold the Lord came with his holy myriads to execute judgment on all, and to convict all the ungodly of all their deeds of ungodliness which they have committed in such an ungodly way, and of all harsh things which ungodly sinners have spoken against him. *John 5:28,29; II Thessalonians 1:8-10; Revelation 20:11-14; Isaiah 26:21; Micah 7:16,17; Psalm 5:5; Psalm 50:1-3; Malachi 3:2,3; Daniel 7:9,10.*

[11]*Matthew 3:12* ...Whose fan is in his hand, and he will thoroughly purge his floor, and gather his wheat into the garner; but he will burn up the chaff with unquenchable fire. *Matthew 13:30* Let both grow together until the harvest: and in the time of harvest, I will say to the reapers, "Gather ye together first the tares, and bind them in bundles to burn them: but gather the wheat into my barn." *Malachi 4:1* For, behold, the day cometh, that shall burn as an oven; and all the proud, yea, and all that do wickedly, shall be stubble: and the day that cometh shall burn them up, saith the Lord of hosts, that it shall leave them neither root nor branch.

[12]*Luke 3:17* ...Whose fan is in his hand, and he will thoroughly purge his floor, and will gather the wheat into his garner; but the chaff he will burn with fire unquenchable.

[13] *I Thessalonians 4:16,17* For the Lord himself shall descend from heaven with a shout, with the voice of the archangel, and with the trump of God: and the dead in Christ shall rise first: Then we which are alive and remain shall be caught up together with them in the clouds, to meet the Lord in the air: and so shall we ever be with the Lord.

[14]*Romans 2:14,15* For when the Gentiles, which have not the law, do by nature the things contained in the law, these, having not the law, are a law unto themselves: Which shew the work of the law written in their hearts, their conscience also bearing witness, and their thoughts the mean while accusing or else excusing one another;...

6

Christian Loses His Burden at the Cross

Now, I saw in my dream that the Highway up which Christian was to go was fenced on either side with a wall that was called Salvation.[1] Up this way, therefore, did burdened Christian run, but not without great difficulty, because of the load on his back.

He ran thus till he came to a place somewhat ascending; and on that place stood a Cross, and a little below, in the bottom, a sepulchre.

So I saw in my dream, that just as Christian came up to the Cross, his burden loosed from off his shoulders, fell from off his back, and began to tumble down the hill, and so it continued to do till it came to the mouth of the sepulchre. There it fell in, and I saw it no more!

Then Christian was glad and lightsome, and said with a merry heart, "He hath given me rest by His sorrow, and life by His death!" He stood still awhile to look and wonder, for it was very surprising to him that the sight of the Cross should thus ease him of his burden. And so he looked, and looked again, until the very springs of his eyes sent water running down his cheeks.[2] Now, as he stood there, looking and

CHRISTIAN'S BURDEN FALLS OFF

weeping, behold three Shining Ones came and saluted him,
saying, "Peace be to you." The first said, "Your sins are
forgiven you."[3] The second Shining One stripped him of his
rags, and placed on him a change of raiment.[4] The third set a
mark in his forehead,[5] and gave him a roll with a seal upon

it, which he instructed him to guard carefully as he ran and to present it at the Celestial Gate when he arrived. So they went their way.

Christian gave three great leaps for joy and went on his way, singing as he went,

Blest cross! Blest grave! Blest rather be
The Man who there was put to death for me!

THE THREE SHINING ONES

In my dream, then, I saw that he went on in this joyful way down the hill. There he saw, a little to one side, three men fast asleep, with fetters upon their heels. The name of one was Simple, of another, Sloth, and of the third, Presumption.

Christian, then, seeing them in this condition, went to them to see if possibly he might awake them and cried, "You are like them that sleep on the top of a mast; awake, therefore, and come away.[6] Be willing, and I will help you off with your irons!" Also he told them, "If he that goeth about like a roaring lion comes by, you will certainly become a prey to his teeth!"[7]

With that they looked at him, and Simple replied, "I see no danger." Sloth said, "Yet a little more sleep." And Presumption added, "Every tub must stand upon his own bottom." And so they went to sleep again, and Christian went on his way. Yet he was troubled to think that men in such danger should so little esteem the kindness in his offer to help them, both by awakening them, counselling them, and offering to help them off with their irons.

As he was troubled about this, he saw two men come tumbling over the wall on the left side of the narrow way. Soon, they hurried and caught up with him. The name of one was Formalist, and of the other, Hypocrisy. As they drew up to him, they began conversing together.

"Gentlemen," asked Christian, "where did you come from, and where are you heading?"

Together they replied, "We were born in the land of Vainglory, and we are going for praise to Mount Zion."

"Then why," Christian continued, "did you not come in at the gate which stands at the beginning of the Way? Do you not know that it is written,'He that cometh not in by the door, but climbeth up some other way, the same is a thief and a robber'?"[8]

FORMALIST

Formalist and Hypocrisy said that to go to the gate for entrance was by all their countrymen counted too far around, and that, therefore, their usual way was to make a shortcut of it, and to climb over the wall as they had done.

Christian countered, "But will it not be counted a trespass against the Lord of the City to which we are going, thus to violate His revealed will?"

Formalist and Hypocrisy told him that, as for that, he need

HYPOCRISY

not trouble his head. For what they did they had custom, and they could produce, if need be, testimony that could witness it for more than a thousand years.

"But," said Christian, "will it stand a trial at law?"

They told him that custom, since it was of such long standing — more than a thousand years — would doubtless now be admitted as a thing legal by an impartial judge.

"And besides," said they, "if we get into the Way, what does it matter which way we get in? If we are in, we are in. You are only in the Way, who, as we perceive, came in at the gate. We are also in the Way, who came tumbling over the wall. So wherein, pray, is your condition better than ours?"

Christian replied: "I walk by the rule of my Master, while you walk by the rude working of your fancies. You are counted as thieves already by the Lord of the Way; therefore, I suspect you will not be found true men at the end of the Way. You came in by yourselves without His direction, and shall go out by yourselves without His mercy."

To this they made him but little answer, and suggested that he look to himself.

I saw then that they went on, every man in his way, without much conferring with one another, except that these two men told Christian that, as to law and ordinances, they did not doubt that they did them as conscientiously as did he. "Therefore," said they, "we do not see wherein you differ from us, except by the coat on your back, which was, as we imagine, given you by some of your neighbors to hide the shame of your nakedness."

"You will not be saved by laws and ordinances, since you did not come in by the door," said Christian.[9] "And as for this coat, it was given me by the Lord of the Place to which I go, in order, as you say, to cover my nakedness. And I take it as a token of His kindness to me, for I had nothing but rags before. This is a comfort to me as I travel. Surely, I think, when I get to the gate of the City, the Lord of it will know me for good, since I have His coat on my back, a coat that He gave me freely in the day when He stripped me of my rags. I have, too, a mark in my forehead, which you may not have noticed, which one of my Lord's most intimate associates placed there the day the burden fell off my shoulders. I tell you, moreover, that I was given then a roll sealed, to comfort me by reading as I go in the Way. I was also told to give it in at the Celestial Gate, to make certain my entry there. I doubt that you have all these things, because you did not come in at the gate.''

They gave him no answer to these things, but looked at each other and laughed. Then as they all went on, Christian walked ahead of them, sometimes sighing as he went, sometimes with good cheer. And as he went, he often read from the roll that one of the Shining Ones gave him, and by it he was refreshed.

Notes on Chapter 6

[1]*Isaiah 26:1* In that day this song will be sung in the land of Judah: ''We have a strong city; he sets up salvation as walls and bulwarks.''

[2]*Zechariah 12:10* ...When they look on him whom they have pierced, they shall mourn for him, as one mourns for an only child, and weep bitterly over him, as one weeps over a first-born.

[3]*Mark 2:5* And when Jesus saw their faith, he said...''My son, your sins are forgiven.''

[4]*Zechariah 3:4* And the angel said to those who were standing before him, ''Remove the filthy garments from him.'' And he said to him, ''Behold, I have taken your iniquity away from you, and I will clothe you with rich apparel.''

[5]*Ephesians 1:13* In him you also, who have heard the word of truth, the gospel of your salvation, and have believed in him, were sealed with the promised Holy Spirit.

[6]*Proverbs 23:34* You will be like one who lies down in the midst of the sea, like one who lies on the top of a mast.

[7]*I Peter 5:8* Be sober, be watchful. Your adversary the devil prowls around like a roaring lion, seeking someone to devour.

[8]*John 10:1*

[9]*Galatians 2:16* ...A man is not justified by works of the law, but through faith in Jesus Christ, even we (Jews) have believed in Christ Jesus... because by works of the law shall no one be justified.

7

The Hill of Difficulty

I beheld then that they all went on till they came to the foot of the Hill Difficulty, at the bottom of which was a spring. There were also in the same place two other ways, besides that which came straight from the gate; one turned to the left and the other to the right, at the bottom of the hill. But the narrow Way lay right up the hill, and the name of that going up the side of the hill is called Difficulty. Christian now went to the spring,[1] and drank of it to refresh himself, and then began to go up the hill, saying:

> *This hill, though high, I covet to ascend;*
> *The difficulty will not me offend,*
> *For I perceive the Way to life lies here.*
> *Come, pluck up, heart, let's neither faint nor fear.*
> *Better, though* difficult, *the right way to go,*
> *Than wrong, though* easy, *where the end is woe.*

Christian's two companions also came to the foot of the hill. But when they saw that the hill was steep and high, and that there were two other ways to go, and supposing also that these two ways might meet again with that up which Christian went, on the other side of the hill, they were resolved to go in those ways. Now the name of the one was Danger, and the name of the other, Destruction. So the one took the way which is called

CHRISTIAN CLIMBING THE HILL OF DIFFICULTY

Danger, which led him into a great wood; and the other went directly up the way to destruction, which led him into a wide field, full of dark mountains, where he stumbled and fell, and rose no more.

I looked then after Christian, to see him go up the hill, where I perceived he went from running to walking, and from walking to clambering on his hands and his knees, because of the steepness of the place. About midway to the top of the hill was a pleasant arbor, made by the Lord of the hill for the refreshment of weary travelers. Here Christian, as he arrived, sat down to rest himself, pulling his roll out of his bosom to read for his comfort as he rested. He also began to look afresh at the coat which had been given to him as he stood by the Cross. Thus pleasing himself a while, he fell into a slumber, and then into a fast sleep, which kept him in that place until it was almost night. In his sleep his roll fell out of his hand. But as he slept, there came one to him and awaked him, saying, "Go to the ant, thou sluggard; consider her ways, and be wise."[2] And with that, Christian suddenly started up, and sped on his way as fast as he could till he came to the top of the hill.

Now when he was got up to the top of the hill, he met two men running at full speed; the name of the one was Timorous, and of the other Mistrust.

"Sirs," said Christian, "what is the matter? You run the wrong way."

Timorous answered that they were going to the City of Zion, and had got up that difficult place. "But," said he, "the farther we go, the more danger we meet with, so we turned and are going back again."

"Yes," said Mistrust, "for just before us lie a couple of lions in the way. Whether they are sleeping or waking, we know not, and we could not think, if we came within their reach, but they would quickly pull us in pieces."

Then Christian spoke: "You make me afraid, but whither

TIMOROUS AND MISTRUST

shall I fly to be safe? If I go back to my own country, that is destined for fire and brimstone, and I shall certainly perish there. If I can get to the Celestial City, I am sure to be in safety there. I must venture! To go back is nothing but death; to go forward is fear of death, and life everlasting beyond it. I will yet go forward!''

So Mistrust and Timorous ran down the hill, and Christian went on his way. But thinking again of what he heard from these men, he felt in his bosom for his roll, and it was not to be found. Then Christian was in great distress and knew not what to do; for he lacked that which used to relieve him and that which was to have been his pass into the Celestial City. Here, therefore, he began to be much perplexed, and knew not what to do. At last he remembered that he had slept in the arbor on the side of the hill, and falling down on his knees, he asked God's forgiveness for that his foolish act. Then he went back to look for his roll.

But all the way back, who can sufficiently set forth the sorrow of Christian's heart? Sometimes he sighed, sometimes he wept, and oftentimes he chided himself for being so foolish to fall asleep in that place which was erected only for a little refreshment from his weariness. Thus, therefore, he went back, carefully looking on this side and on that, all the way as he went, if happily he might find his roll that had been his comfort so many times in his journey. He went back thus till he came again within sight of the arbor where he had sat and slept. But that sight renewed his sorrow the more, by bringing fresh to his mind his evil of sleeping.[3] Thus, therefore, he now went on bewailing his sinful sleep, saying, "O wretched man that I am! that I should sleep in the daytime! that I should sleep in the midst of difficulty! that I should so indulge the flesh as to use that rest for ease to my flesh, which the Lord of the hill hath erected only for the relief of the spirits of pilgrims!

"How many steps have I taken in vain! Thus it happened to Israel, for their sin they were sent back again by the way of the Red Sea, and I am made to tread these steps with sorrow which I might have trodden with delight, had it not been for this sinful sleep. How far might I have been on my way by this time! I am made to tread those steps thrice over which I needed not to have trodden but once. Yes, and now I am likely to be kept overnight, for the day is almost spent. Oh, that I had not slept!"

By this time he had come back to the arbor again, where for a while he sat down and wept. But, at last, looking sorrowfully down under the seat, he spied his roll! With trembling and haste, he caught it up and put it in his bosom. But who can tell how joyful this man was when he had gotten his roll again! For this roll was the assurance of his life and acceptance at the desired haven. Therefore he laid it up in his bosom, gave thanks to God for directing his eye to the place where it lay, and with joy and tears betook himself again to his journey. But oh, how nimbly now did he go up the rest of the hill! Yet before he got up, the sun went down upon Christian, and this made him again recall the folly of his sleeping to his remembrance. He began to commiserate with himself: "O sinful sleep: how for your sake, am I likely to be overtaken by darkness on my journey! I must walk without the sun; darkness must cover the path of my feet; and I must hear the noise of the frightful creatures because of my sinful sleep."[4] Now also he remembered the story that Mistrust and Timorous had told him, how they were frightened by the sight of the lions. Christian said to himself, "These beasts range at night for their prey, and if they should meet me in the dark, how can I avoid them? How can I escape being torn to pieces?"

Thus he went on his way.

Notes on Chapter 7

[1]*Isaiah 49:10* They shall not hunger nor thirst; neither shall the heat nor sun smite them: for he that hath mercy on them shall lead them, even by the springs of water shall he guide them.

[2]*Proverbs 6:6*

[3]*Revelation 2:5* Remember then from what you have fallen; repent and do the works you did at first. If not, I will come to you and remove your lampstand from its place, unless you repent. *I Thessalonians 5:7,8* For those who sleep, sleep at night; and those who get drunk are drunk at night. But since we belong to the day, let us be sober, and put on the breastplate of faith and love, and for a helmet, the hope of salvation.

[4]*I Thessalonians 5:6* So then, let us not sleep as others do, but let us keep awake and be sober.

8
The House Beautiful

While Christian was bewailing his unhappy failure, he lifted up his eyes and saw before him a very stately palace, the name of which was Beautiful; and it stood just by the side of the highway.

So he made haste and went forward, to see if he might find lodging there. Before he had gone far, he entered into a very narrow passage, which was about two hundred yards from the Porter's lodge.[1] Looking very closely before him as he went, Christian espied two lions in the way.

"Now," thought he, "I see the dangers that drove Mistrust and Timorous back." The lions were chained, but he could not see the chains. Then he was afraid, and even thought about going back after Timorous and Mistrust, for he feared that nothing but death was before him. But the Porter of the lodge, whose name is Watchful, perceiving that Christian made a halt as if he would go back, cried to him saying, "Is your strength so small?[2] Fear not the lions, for they are chained, and are placed there for trial of faith, where it is, and to reveal those who have none. Keep in the midst of the path and no hurt shall come to you."

Then I saw that he went on, trembling for fear of the lions, but taking good heed to the directions of the Porter; he heard them roar, but they did him no harm. Then he clapped his hands and went on till he came and stood before the gate where the Porter was.

Christian said to Porter, "Sir, what house is this, and may I lodge here tonight?"

The Porter answered, "This house was built by the Lord of the hill, and he built it for the relief and security of pilgrims." The Porter then asked whence he was and whither he was going.

"I am come from the City of Destruction, and am going to Mount Zion; but because the sun is now set, I desire, if I may, to lodge here tonight."

"What is your name?"

"My name is now Christian, but my name at the first was Graceless."

"But how does it happen that you come so late? The sun is set," asked the Porter.

"I would have been here sooner, except that, wretched man that I am, I slept in the arbor that stands of the hillside," replied Christian. "No, even so, I would have been here much sooner if I had not in my sleep lost my evidence, and came without it to the top of the hill; then feeling for it, and not finding it, I was forced with sorrow of heart to go back to the place where I slept, where I found it; and now I am here."

"Well, I will call out one of the virgins of this place, who will, if she likes your talk, take you into the rest of the family according to the rules of the house." So Watchful, the Porter, rang a bell, and at its sound there came out at the door of the house a grave and beautiful damsel, named Discretion, who asked why she had been called.

The Porter answered, "This man is on a journey from the

CHRISTIAN AT THE DOOR OF PALACE BEAUTIFUL

City of Destruction to Mount Zion, but being weary and over-taken by darkness, has asked if he might lodge here tonight. I told him that after you have talked with him, you may do as seems good to you, even according to the law of the house.''

The damsel then asked Christian where he had come from

and where he was going, and he told her. Then she asked him what he had seen and met with in the Way, and he told her. And last, she asked his name.

"It is Christian," he said, "and I have so much the more a desire to lodge here tonight, because by what I perceive, this place was built by the Lord of the hill, for the relief and security of pilgrims."

So she smiled, but tears stood in her eyes; and after a little pause, she said, "I will call two or three more of the family." So she ran to the door, and called out Prudence, Piety and Charity, who, after a little more discourse with him, welcomed him into the family. Many of them, meeting him at the threshold of the house, said, "Come in, blessed of the Lord; this house was built by the Lord of the hill, for the purpose of entertaining such pilgrims." Bowing his head, he followed them into the house. When he was inside, they gave him something to drink, and agreed together that until supper was ready, some of them should have some conversation with Christian, for the best use of the time. And they appointed Piety, Prudence and Charity to discourse with him.

Piety began, saying: "Come, good Christian, since we have been so loving to you to receive you in our house this night, let us, if perhaps we may better ourselves, talk with you of the things that have happened to you in your pilgrimage."

"With a very good will, and I am glad that you are so well disposed," he answered.

"What moved you at first to commit yourself to a pilgrim's life?" asked Piety.

"I was driven out of my native country by a sound that came into my ears," said Christian. "It was the word that if I stayed in that place where I was, certain destruction awaited me."

"But how did it happen that you came out of your country this way?" she asked.

"It was as God would have it," was his reply. "When I was under the fears of destruction, I did not know where to go. By chance there came a man to me as I was trembling and weeping. His name was Evangelist, and he directed me to the wicket gate; otherwise I should never have found it. It was he who set me into the Way that has led me directly to this house."

"But," Piety continued, "did you not come by the house of the Interpreter?"

"Yes, and I saw such things that I will remember them as long as I live; especially three things: first, how Christ, in spite of Satan, maintains his work of grace in the heart; second, how the man had sinned himself quite out of hopes of God's mercy; and also the dream of the man who thought in his sleep that the Day of Judgment had come."

"Why, did you hear him tell his dream?" asked Piety.

"Yes, and a dreadful one it was! I thought it made my heart ache as he was telling about it. Yet I am glad I heard it."

"Was that all you saw at the house of the Interpreter?"

"No," said Christian. "He took me and showed me a stately palace, and the people in it were clad in gold. Then there came a venturous man cutting his way through the armed men who stood in the door to keep him out; and I saw that he was then invited to come in and win eternal glory. The thought of those things ravished my heart! I would have stayed at that good man's house a year, but I knew that I had further to go."

"What else did you see in the way?" asked the damsel.

"Saw!" exclaimed Christian. "Why, I went but a little further and I saw one, as I thought in my mind, hang bleeding upon the tree; and the very sight of him made my burden fall off my back (for I had groaned under a very heavy burden). But then, it fell down from me. It was a strange thing to me, for I never saw such a thing before. Yes, and while I stood looking up (for I could not keep from looking), three Shining Ones came to me. One of them testified that my sins were forgiven; another stripped me of my rags, and gave me this broidered coat which you see; and the third set the mark which you see in my forehead, and gave me this sealed roll. And with that he plucked it out of his bosom.

Piety placed another question: "You saw more than this, did you not?"

"The things that I have told you were the best," was Christian's response. "Yet there were some other things I saw. There were three men, Simple, Sloth and Presumption, lying asleep a little out of the way as I came along, with irons on their feet. But do you think that I could awake them? I also met Formality and Hypocrisy, who came tumbling in over the wall, to go, as they pretended, to Zion. They were quickly lost, however, even as I had tried to tell them they would be, but they would not listen or believe. Above all, I found it hard work to get up this hill, and as hard to come by the lions' mouths. Truly, if it had not been for the good man, the Porter who stands at the gate, I do not know but that after all I might have gone back again. But now, I thank God that I am here, and I thank you for receiving me."

Prudence then asked him a few questions and desired an answer from him.

"Do you not think sometimes of the country you came from?" she asked.

"Yes," he replied, "but with shame and detestation. Truly, if I had been mindful of that country from which I came, I might have had an opportunity to return. But now I desire a better country, a heavenly one."[3]

"Do you not yet carry with you some of the things that you were accustomed to associate with?" asked Prudence.

"Yes, but greatly against my will; especially my inward and

carnal thoughts, with which all my countrymen, as well as myself, were delighted; but now all those things are my grief; and if I could but choose my own things, I would choose never to think of those things any more; but when I would be doing that which is best, that which is worst is with me."[4]

"Do you not find sometimes as if those things were vanquished which at other times are your perplexity?"

"Yes, but that is seldom; but they are to me golden hours in which such things happen to me," said Christian.

Prudence went on, "Can you remember by what means you find your annoyances to seem as if they were vanquished?"

"Yes," he answered, "it is when I think of what I saw at the Cross — that will do it; and when I look upon my broidered coat, that will do it; also when I look into the roll that I carry in my bosom, that will do it; and when my thoughts wax warm about the place where I am going, that will do it."

"And what is it that makes you so eager to go to Mount Zion?" she asked.

"Why, there I hope to see Him alive who hung dead on that Cross; and there I hope to be rid of all those things in me that to this day are an annoyance to me; there, they say, there is no death; and there I shall dwell with such company as I like best.[5] For, to tell you the truth, I love Him, because I was eased of my burden by Him, and I am weary of my inward sickness. I should like to be where I shall die no more, with the company of them who shall continually cry, 'Holy, Holy, Holy!' "

Then said Charity to Christian, "Have you a family? Are you a married man?"

"I have a wife and four small children," he answered.

"And why did you not bring them along with you?" she inquired.

Then Christian wept, and said, "Oh, how willingly would

I have done it! But they were all of them completely averse to my going on pilgrimage."

But Charity persisted. "You should have talked to them, and you should have tried to show them the danger of being left behind."

"So I did," he insisted. "I told them also what God had shown me about the destruction of our city. But I seemed to them as one who mocked, and they did not believe me."[6]

"And did you pray to God that he would bless your words of counsel to them?"

"Yes, and that with much affection. For you must know that my wife and poor children were very dear to me."

"But did you tell them of your own sorrow, and fear of destruction? For I suppose that destruction was visible enough to you," said Charity.

"Yes," he replied sadly. "Over and over and over. They could see my fears in my face, in my tears, and in my trembling at the thought of the judgment which hung over our heads. But all this was not sufficient to prevail with them to come with me."

"But what could they say for themselves as to why they did not come?" she asked.

Christian looked at her sadly again. "My wife was afraid of losing this world, and my children were given to the foolish delights of youth. And so, what by one thing and what by another, they left me to wander in this manner alone."

"But did you not, with your vain and empty life, dampen all you said to persuade them to come away with you?"

"Indeed, I cannot commend my life," said Christian. "I am conscious of many failings in it. I know also that a man by his way of life may soon overthrow what by argument or persuasion he tries hard to give others for their good. Yet this I can say: I was very careful not to make them averse to my going on pilgrimage by any unseemly action on my part. Indeed, for this very thing they would tell me that I was too precise, and that I denied myself of things, for their sakes, in which they saw no evil. No, I think I may say that if what they saw in me was an hindrance to them, it was my great fear of sinning against God or of doing any wrong to my neighbor."

"Indeed Cain hated his brother," Charity observed, "because his own works were evil and his brother's righteous";[7] and if your wife and children have been offended with you for these things, then they show that they are not to be persuaded or moved by your entreaties for their own good. Therefore you have delivered your soul from their blood."[8]

Now I saw in my dream that they sat talking together in this way until supper was ready. So when they had made ready, they all sat down to eat. The table was furnished "with fat things, and with wine well refined";[9] and all their talk at the table was about the Lord of the hill, about what He had done and why He did what He did, and why He had built that house. By what they said, I perceived that He had been a great warrior, and had fought with and slain "him that had the power of death," but not without great danger to Himself, which made me love Him the more.[10]

"For, as they said, and as I believe," said Christian, "He did it with the loss of much blood; but that which put glory of grace into all He did was that He did it out of pure love of His country."

Besides, some of the household said they had been with Him and had spoken with Him after He died on the Cross; and they have attested that they had it from His own lips, that He is such a lover of poor pilgrims that the like is not to be found from the East to the West.

They gave him, moreover, an instance of what they affirmed: that He had stripped Himself of His glory, that He might do this for the poor; and that they had heard Him say and affirm "that He would not dwell in the mountain of Zion alone." They said, too, that He had made many pilgrims princes, even though by nature they were beggars born, and their origin had been the dunghill.[11]

Thus they talked on together till late at night; and after they had committed themselves to their Lord for protection, they went to rest: the Pilgrim they assigned to a large upper chamber with its window opening toward the sunrising, which was named Peace; there he slept till the break of day.

In the morning they all got up, and after some more discourse, they told him that he should not leave till they had shown him the rarities of that place. First they took him into the study, where they showed him records of the greatest antiquity. In these they pointed out first the lineage of the Lord of the hill, that He was the son of the Ancient of Days, and that He was begotten before all ages. Here also were more complete records of the acts that He had done, and the names of many hundreds He had taken into His service. Here, too, he saw that He had placed His servants in such dwellings that neither by length of days nor by the decays of nature could they be dissolved.

Then they read to him some of the worthy acts that some of His servants had done; such as how they had "subdued kingdoms, wrought righteousness, obtained promises, stopped the mouths of lions, quenched the violence of fire, escaped the edge of the sword, out of weakness had been made strong, waxed valiant in fight, and turned to flight the armies of the aliens."[12]

They read again, in another part of the records of the house where it showed how willing their Lord was to receive into His favor any, even though they in time past had offered great affronts and offence to His person and His will. Here also were several other histories of many other famous things, which

Christian saw — things both ancient and modern, together with prophecies and predictions of things that will have their certain accomplishment, both to the dread and amazement of enemies, and the comfort and solace of pilgrims.

CHRISTIAN INSTRUCTED AT PALACE BEAUTIFUL

The next day they took him into the armory. There they showed him all manner of equipment which their Lord had provided for pilgrims — sword, shield, helmet, breastplate, all-prayer and shoes that would not wear out. And there was here enough of this to equip as many men for the service of their Lord as there are stars in the heaven.[13]

They also showed him instruments with which some of the Lord's servants had done wonderful things. They showed him

Moses' rod; the hammer and nail with which Jael slew Sisera; the pitchers, trumpets and lamps with which Gideon put to flight the armies of Midian. Then they showed him the ox-goad with which Shamgar slew six hundred men, and the jawbone with which Samson did such mighty feats. They showed him, moreover, the sling and stone with which David slew the giant, Goliath; and the sword with which their Lord will kill the Man of Sin in the day when He shall rise up to the prey. Besides these, they showed him many other excellent things with which he was much delighted. This done, they all went to their rest again.

The following day Christian wanted to move on, but they prevailed on him to stay one more day, because, they said, "if the day is clear, we will show you the Delectable Mountains." They assured him that this view would further add to his comfort, because these mountains were nearer the desired haven than the place where Christian was at present. So he consented and stayed. Next day they took him to the top of the house and bid him look south. As he did so, he saw at a great distance a most pleasant mountainous country, beautified with woods, vineyards, fruits of all sorts, and with flowers, with springs and fountains, very delectable to behold.[14] He asked the name of the country. They said it was Immanuel's Land; "and it is as common," said they, "as this hill is, to and for all the pilgrims.[15] And when you come there from here," said they, "you may see the gate of the Celestial City, as the Shepherds who live there will show you."

Christian was eager to set forward again, and they were willing that he should. "But first," said they, "let us go again into the armory." So they did; and when they came there, they equipped him from head to foot with what had been tested, lest, perhaps, he should meet with assaults in the Way. After Christian had been fitted with his armor, he walked out with his friends to the gate, and there he asked the Porter if he had seen any pilgrims pass by. The Porter answered, "Yes."

"Pray, did you know him?" said he.

"I asked him his name, and he told me it was Faithful."

"Oh," said Christian, "I know him. He is my townsman, my near neighbor. He comes from the place where I was born. How far do you think he may be before?"

"By this time he is below the hill," replied the Porter.

CHRISTIAN GOES DOWN INTO THE VALLEY OF HUMILIATION

"Well," said Christian, "good Porter, the Lord be with you and add to all your blessings much increase, for the kindness you have shown me."

Then he started out, but Discretion, Piety, Charity and Prudence wanted to go with him to the foot of the hill. So they accompanied him, reiterating their former talks, till they came to go down the hill. Then said Christian, "As it was difficult coming up, so, as far as I can see, it is dangerous going down."

"Yes," said Prudence, "so it is, for it is a hard matter for a man to go down into the Valley of Humiliation, as you are now, and not to slip on the way."

"That is why," they said, "we came out to accompany you down the hill."

So he began to go down, but very warily; yet in spite of all, his foot slipped once or twice.

Then I saw in my dream that these good companions, when Christian had reached the bottom of the hill, gave him a loaf of bread, a bottle of wine, and a cluster of raisins; and then he went on his way.

Notes on Chapter 8

[1]Bunyan's word here is *a furlong.*

[2]*Mark 13:34-37*

[3]*Hebrews 11:15,16* If they had been thinking of that land from which they had gone out, they would have had opportunity to return. But as it is, they desire a better country, that is, a heavenly one. Therefore God is not ashamed to be called their God, for he has prepared for them a city.

[4] *Romans 7*

[5]*Isaiah 25:8* He will swallow up death for ever, and the Lord God will wipe away tears from all faces, and the reproach of his people he will take away from all the earth; for the Lord has spoken. *Revelation 21:4* He will wipe away every tear from their eyes, and death shall be no more, neither shall there

be mourning nor crying nor pain any more, for the former things have passed away.

[6]*Genesis 19:14* So Lot went out and said to his sons-in-law, who were to marry his daughters, "Up, get out of this place; for the Lord is about to destroy the city." But he seemed to his sons-in-law to be jesting.

[7]*I John 3:12* And be not like Cain who was of the evil one and murdered his brother. And why did he murder him? Because his own deeds were evil and his brother's righteous.

[8]*Ezekiel 3:19* But if you warn the wicked, and he does not turn from his wickedness, or from his wicked way, he shall die in his iniquity; but you will have saved your life.

[9]*Isaiah 25:6* On this mountain the Lord of hosts will make for all peoples a feast of fat things, a feast of wine on the lees, of fat things full of marrow, of wine on the lees well refined.

[10]*Hebrews 2:14,15* Since therefore the children share in flesh and blood, he himself likewise partook of the same nature, that through death he might destroy him who has the power of death, that is, the devil, and deliver all those who through fear of death were subject to lifelong bondage.

[11]*I Samuel 2:8* He raises up the poor from the dust; he lifts the needy from the ash heap, to make them sit with princes and inherit a seat of honor.... *Psalm 113:7* He raises the poor from the dust, and lifts the needy from the ash heap, to make them sit with princes, with the princes of his people.

[12]*Hebrews 11:33,34*

[13]*Ephesians 6:11-17*

[14]*Isaiah 33:16,17* He will dwell on the heights; his place of defense will be the fortress of the rocks; his bread will be given him, his water will be sure. Your eyes will see the king in his beauty; they will behold a land that stretches afar.

[15] *Common* here means available to all.

9

The Valley of Humiliation

N ow, in this Valley of Humiliation, poor Christian was hard put to it. For he had gone but a little way before he saw a foul fiend coming over the field to meet him. His name is Apollyon. Christian began to be afraid, and to wonder in his mind whether to go back or to stand his ground. But he considered again that he had no armor for his back; and therefore thought that to turn the back to him might give him greater advantage and enable him to pierce him with his darts with ease. So he resolved to venture and stand his ground. "For," thought he, "had I no more in my mind than the saving of my life, this would be the best way to stand."

So he went on, and Apollyon met him. Now the monster was hideous to behold. He was clothed with scales, like a fish (and they are his pride); he had wings like a dragon, feet like a bear, and out of his belly came fire and smoke, and his mouth was the mouth of a lion.

When he had come up to Christian, he looked at him with a disdainful countenance, and began to question him in this way: "Where do you come from, and where are you going?"

"I have come from the City of Destruction," answered

Christian, "which is the place of all evil, and I am going to the City of Zion."

Apollyon retorted, "By this I see you are one of my subjects, for all that country is mine, and I am the prince and god of it. How is it, then, that you have run away from your king? Were it not that I hope you may do me more service, I would strike you now, with one blow, to the ground!"

"I was born, indeed, in your dominions," Christian replied, "but your service was hard, and your wages such that a man could not live on, 'for the wages of sin is death.'[1] Therefore when I had come of age, I did as other circumspect people do. I looked out to see if, perhaps I might improve myself."

"There is no prince who will so lightly lose his subjects," replied Apollyon, "and neither will I as yet lose you. But since you complain of your service and wages, be content to go back, and what our country can afford, I promise I will give you."

Christian answered: "But I have given myself to another, even the King of princes; so how can I, with fairness, go back with you now?"

"You have acted according to the old saying, 'Changed a bad for a worse,' " Apollyon wheedled. "But it is ordinary for those that have professed themselves His servants, after a while to give Him the slip, and return again to me. Do this yourself, and all will be well."

"But I have given Him my promise, and sworn my allegiance to Him," protested Christian. "How then can I go back from this, and not be hanged as a traitor?"

Pretending to be merciful, Apollyon murmured, "You did the same to me, and yet I am willing to overlook all, if now you will turn again and go back into my service."

Christian stood his ground. "What I promised you was before I was of age; and besides, I count the Prince under whose banner now I stand is able to absolve me; yes, and to pardon what I did in my compliance with you. And besides, O destroying Apollyon! To speak truth, I like His service, His wages, His servants, His government, His company and country better than yours. Therefore, stop trying to persuade me any further. I am His servant and I will follow Him.''

''Consider again when you are in a cooler state of mind,'' the enemy continued, ''what you are most likely to meet with in the way you are going. You know that, for the most part, His servants came to an ill end, because they are transgressors against me and my ways. How many of them have been put to shameful deaths? And besides, you count His service better than mine, when as a matter of fact, He never came from the place where He dwells to deliver any who served Him out of the hands of their enemies. But as for me, how many times, as all the world very well knows, have I delivered, either by power or fraud, those who have faithfully served me, from Him and His, even though they were taken by them. And so I will deliver you.''

Christian said, ''His forbearance at present to deliver them is on purpose to try their love, whether they will cleave to Him to the end; and as for the ill end you say they come to, that is most glorious in their account. As for present deliverance, they do not much expect it, for they stay for their glory and then they shall have it, when their Prince comes in His glory and the glory of the angels.''

''You have already been unfaithful in your service to Him; how do you think to receive wages from Him?'' asked Apollyon.

''Wherein, O Apollyon! have I been unfaithful to Him?'' asked Christian, somewhat taken aback.

''You fainted at your beginning, when you were almost choked in the Gulf of Despond. You attempted wrong ways to be rid of your burden, when you should have stayed till your

Prince had taken it off. You sinfully slept and lost your choice thing. You were, also, almost persuaded to go back at the sight of the lions. And when you talk of your journey and what you have heard and seen, you are inwardly desirous of vain-glory in all you say and do.''

CHRISTIAN DEFEATS APOLLYON

"All this is true," admitted Christian, "and much more which you have left out. But the Prince whom I serve and honor is merciful and ready to forgive; but, besides, these infirmities possessed me in your country. I have groaned under them, been sorry for them, and have obtained pardon of my Prince."[2]

Then Apollyon broke out in a grievous rage, saying, "I am an enemy to this Prince; I hate His person, His laws, and His people! I have come out purposely to withstand you!"

"Apollyon, beware what you do!" retorted Christian. "For I am in the King's highway, the way of holiness! Therefore, take heed to yourself!"

Then Apollyon straddled quite over the whole breadth of the way, and said, "I have no fear in this matter! Prepare yourself to die, for I swear by my infernal den that you shall go no further! Here I will spill your soul!"

With that he threw a flaming dart at Christian's breast; but Christian had a shield in his hand, with which he caught it, and so avoided being damaged by it. Then Christian saw it was time to bestir himself, so he quickly began to move. Apollyon, just as fast, came at him, throwing darts as thick as hail. Notwithstanding all that Christian could do to avoid it, Apollyon wounded him in his head, his hand and foot. This made Christian retreat a little; and Apollyon followed his work at full speed. Christian again took courage and resisted as manfully as he could. This sore combat lasted for more than half a day, till Christian was almost exhausted. For you can realize that Christian, because of his wounds, was growing weaker and weaker.

Apollyon, seeing his opportunity, began to draw up close to Christian, and wrestling with him, gave him a dreadful fall. With that, Christian's sword flew out of his hand. Then said Apollyon, "I am sure of you now!" With that he had almost pressed him to death, so that Christian began to despair of his life. But, as God would have it, while Apollyon was readying for his final blow, to make a full end of this good man, Christian nimbly stretched out his hand for his sword, caught it and said, "Rejoice not against me, O mine enemy; when I fall I shall arise!"[3] With that he gave him a deadly thrust, which made him fall back as one who had received a deadly wound. Christian seeing this, made at him again saying, "Nay, in all these things we are more than conquerors through Him that loved us."[4] With that, Apollyon spread forth his dragon's wings and sped away, so that Christian for a season saw him no more.[5]

In this fight no man can imagine, unless he had seen and heard it as I did, what yelling and hideous roaring Apollyon made all during the fight. He spoke like a dragon. Nor can one imagine, on the other side, what sighs and groans burst from Christian's heart. I never saw him all the while give so much as one pleasant look, until he perceived that he had wounded Apollyon with his two-edged sword. Then, indeed, he did smile and look upward. But it was the most dreadful sight that ever I saw!

> *A more unequal match can hardly be —*
> Christian *must fight an Angel; but you see,*
> *The valiant man, by handling Sword and Shield,*
> *Doth make him, though a dragon, quit the field.*

When the battle was over, Christian said, "I will here give thanks to him who delivered me out of the mouth of the lion, to Him who helped me against Apollyon."

Then there came to him a hand with some of the leaves of the tree of life, which Christian took, and applied to the wounds that he had received in the battle, and he was healed

CHRISTIAN RETURNS THANKS FOR VICTORY

immediately. Sitting down in that place, he ate bread and drank of the bottle which had been given him a little while before, and so, being refreshed, he addressed himself to his journey with his sword drawn in his hand; for he said, "I know not but that some other enemy may be at hand." But he met with no other affront from Apollyon all the way through this valley.

Now at the end of this valley was another, called the Valley of the Shadow of Death, and Christian must needs go through it, because the way to the Celestial City lay through the midst of it. Now this valley is a very solitary place. The prophet Jeremiah thus describes it: "A wilderness, a land of deserts and of pits, a land of drought, and of the shadow of death, a land that no man passed through and where no man dwelt."[6]

Now here Christian was worse put to it than in his fight with Apollyon, as by the sequel you shall see.

Notes on Chapter 9

[1] *Romans 6:23*

[2] Here is one of Satan's favorite weapons against a Christian — the suggestion that he has not been forgiven his sins. Here is the way Bunyan describes it in *The Jerusalem Sinner Saved* and *Christ's Love and the Saint's Knowledge*: "Satan is loathe to part with a great sinner. What, my true servant, quoth he, my old servant, wilt thou forsake me now? Having so often sold thyself to me to work wickedness, wilt thou forsake me now? Thou horrible wretch, dost not know that thou hast sinned thyself beyond the reach of grace, and dost thou think to find mercy now? Art not thou a murderer, a thief, a harlot, a witch, a sinner of the greatest size, and dost thou look for mercy now? Dost thou think that Christ will foul his fingers with thee? It is enough to make angels blush, saith Satan, to see so vile a one knock at heaven's gates for mercy, and wilt thou be so abominably bold to do it? Thus Satan dealt with me, says the great sinner, when at first I came to Jesus Christ. And what did you reply? saith the tempted. Why, I granted the whole charge to be true, says the other. And what, did you despair, or how? No, saith he, I said I am Magdalene, I am Zaccheus, I am the thief, I am the harlot, I am the publican, I am the prodigal, and one of Christ's murderers — yea, worse than any of these; and yet God was so far off from rejecting of me, as I found afterwards, that there was music and dancing in his house for me, and for joy that I was come home unto him." When Satan charged Luther with a long list of crimes, he replied, This is all true; but write another line at the bottom, "The blood of Jesus Christ his Son cleanseth us from all sin."

[3] *Micah 7:8*

[4] *Romans 8:37*

[5] *James 4:7b* Resist the devil and he will flee from you.

[6] *Jeremiah 2:6*

10

The Valley of the Shadow of Death

I saw then in my dream, that when Christian had reached the borders of the Shadow of Death, two men met him, children of those who brought up an evil report of the good land, making haste to go back.[1]

"Where are you going?" asked Christian.

They said, "Back! Back! and we would have you do so, too, if you prize either life or peace."

"Why, what's the matter?"

"Matter?" said they. "We were going the same way you are heading, and went as far as we dared. Indeed, we were almost beyond coming back; for had we gone a little further, we would not be here to bring the news to you."

"But what have you met with?"

"Why, we were almost in the Valley of the Shadow of Death but by happy chance, we looked before us and saw the danger before we came to it," they answered.[2]

"But what have you seen?" said Christian.

"Seen!" they exclaimed. "Why the Valley itself, which is dark as pitch! We also saw hobgoblins, satyrs and dragons of the pit, and we heard in that Valley a continual howling and yelling, as from people in unutterable misery who sat bound in affliction and irons. Over the Valley hang the discouraging clouds of confusion. Death also always spreads his wings over it. In a word, it is dreadful in every way, being utterly without order."[3]

"Then," said Christian, "I perceive by what you have said that this is my way to the desired haven."[4]

"Have it your way!" they retorted. "We will not choose it for ours!"

So they parted, and Christian went on his way, but still with his sword drawn in his hand, for fear that he should be assaulted.

I saw then in my dream so far as this valley reached, there was on the right hand a very deep ditch. That ditch is the one into which the blind have been led in all ages and have there miserably perished.[5] Again, behold, on the left hand there was a very dangerous marsh into which, if even a good man falls, he can find no bottom for his foot to stand on. Into that bog King David once fell, and no doubt would have suffocated in it if He who is able had not plucked him out.[6]

The pathway here was exceedingly narrow, and because of this, good Christian was the more put to it; for when he sought, in the dark, to shun the ditch on the one hand, he was ready to tip over into the mire on the other; also when he sought to escape the mire, without great carefulness he would be ready to fall into the ditch. Thus he went on, and I heard him here sigh bitterly; for, besides the dangers mentioned above, the pathway here was so dark that ofttimes when he picked up his foot to go forward, he did not know where or upon what he would set it next.

About the midst of this Valley, I perceived the mouth of hell to be, and it stood also close by the wayside. "Now," thought Christian, "what shall I do?" And every now and then the flame and smoke would come out in such abundance, with sparks and hideous noises (things that did not care for Christian's sword as Apollyon did beforehand), that Christian was forced to put up his sword and betake himself to another weapon, called All-prayer.[7] So he cried in my hearing, ''O Lord, I beseech thee, deliver my soul!''[8] He went on in this manner a

THE VALLEY OF THE SHADOW OF DEATH

111

great while, but still the flames continue to reach towards him.[9] He heard, too, doleful voices and rushings to and fro, so that sometimes he thought he would be torn to pieces or trodden down like mire in the streets. This frightful sight was seen and those dreadful noises were heard by him for several miles together. Coming to a place where he thought he heard a company of fiends coming to meet him, he stopped, and began to muse what he best should do. Sometimes he had half a thought to go back. Then again he thought he might be halfway through the valley. He remembered also how he had already vanquished many a danger, and that the danger of going back might be much more than to go forward. So he resolved to go on. Yet the fiends seemed to come nearer and nearer, but when they were almost at him, he cried out with a most vehement voice, "I will walk in the strength of the Lord God!"[10] So they backed up and came no further.

One thing I would not let slip. I took notice that now poor Christian was so confounded that he did not know his own voice. This is how I understood it: just when he was come over to the mouth of the burning pit, one of the wicked ones got behind him, stepped up softly to him, and whispered many grievous blasphemies to him. Poor Christian verily thought these had proceeded from his own mind. This put him into greater conflict than anything that he had met before, even to think that he should now blaspheme Him whom he loved so much before. Yet, if he could have helped it, he would not have done it, but he had not the discretion either to stop his ears, or to know from whence these blasphemies came.

When Christian had traveled in this disconsolate condition some considerable time, he thought he heard the voice of a man as if going before him, saying, "Though I walk through the valley of the shadow of death, I will fear no evil, for thou art with me."[11]

Then he was glad for these reasons: —

First, because he gathered from this that others who feared God were in this valley as well as himself.

Secondly, he perceived that God was with them, though in that dark and dismal state. "And why not," thought he, "with me? Though, for the difficulties of this place, I cannot perceive it."[12]

Thirdly, he hoped, could he overtake them, to have company by and by.

So he went on, and called to the one whose voice he heard before him, but that one himself did not know how to answer him, because he thought to himself, too, to be alone. By and by the day broke. Then said Christian, "He hath turned the shadow of death into the morning."[13]

Now when morning had come, Christian looked back — not out of desire to return, but to see by the light of day what hazards he had gone through in the dark. He saw more perfectly the ditch that was on the one hand and the mire that was on the other. He saw, too, how narrow the way was which led between them both, as well as the hobgoblins, satyrs, and dragons of the pit. But they were all far off now, for after the break of day they would not come near him. Yet they were made visible to him according to that which is written, "He discovereth deep things out of darkness, and bringeth out to light the shadow of death."[14]

Christian was very moved with his deliverance from all the dangers of his solitary way. Those dangers, though he had feared them more before, he saw more clearly now because the light of day made them visible to him. About this time the sun was rising, and this was another mercy to Christian. For you must note that though the first part of the Valley of the Shadow of Death was very dangerous, this second part which he was yet to go, was, if possible, far more dangerous. From the place where he now stood, all the way to the end of the valley, the way was set full of snares, traps, devices and nets

CHRISTIAN ENTERS THE SECOND PART OF THE VALLEY OF THE
SHADOW OF DEATH

here and so full of pits, pitfalls, deep holes and shelvings down
there, that, if it had now been as dark as it had been in the first
part of the way, even though he had a thousand souls, they
would have, in all probability, been thrown away. But, as
I said just now, the sun was rising!

Then he said, "His candle shineth upon my head and by his light I walk through darkness."[15]

In this light he came to the end of the valley.

Notes on Chapter 10

[1]*Numbers 13:32*

[2]*Psalms 44:19* That thou shouldst have broken us in the place of jackals, and covered us with deep darkness. *Psalm 107:10* Some sat in darkness and gloom, prisoners in afflictions and irons.

[3]*Job 3:5* Let gloom and deep darkness claim it. Let clouds dwell upon it: let the blackness of the day terrify it. *Job 10:22* The land of gloom and chaos, where light is as darkness.

[4]*Jeremiah 2:6* They did not say, "Where is the Lord who brought us up from the land of Egypt, who led us in the wilderness in a land of deserts and pits, in a land of drought and deep darkness..."

[5]*Psalm 69:14,15* With thy faithful help rescue me from sinking in the mire; let me be delivered from my enemies and from the deep waters. Let not the flood sweep over me, or the deep swallow me up, or the pit close its mouth over me.

[6]*Psalm 40:2* He drew me up from the desolate pit, out of the miry bog, and set my feet upon a rock, making my steps secure.

[7]*Ephesians 6:18* Pray at all times in the Spirit, with all prayer and supplication.

[8]*Psalm 116:4*

[9] "The sight of an immortal soul in peril of its eternal interests, beset with enemies, engaged in a desperate conflict, with hell opening her mouth before, and fiends and temptations pressing after, is a sublime and awful spectacle. Man cannot aid him; all his help is in God only." *(Cheever)*

[10]*Psalm 71:16*

[11]*Psalm 23:4*

[12]*Job 9:11* Lo, he passes by me and I see him not; he moves on, but I do not perceive him.

[13]*Amos 5:8*

[14]*Job 12:22*

[15]*Job 29:3*

II

Faithful's Testimony

As Christian went on his way, he came to a small hill which had been made so that pilgrims might see before them. Christian went up, and looking forward saw Faithful before him upon his journey. Christian called out loudly, "Ho! ho! soho! wait, and I will be your companion!"

At that Faithful looked behind him, as Christian cried again, "Stay! stay till I come up to you!" But Faithful answered, "No, I am running for my life; and the avenger of blood is behind me."

At this, Christian summoned all his strength and quickly caught up with Faithful, and actually ran beyond him. So the last was first. Christian then smiled vain-gloriously, because he had gotten ahead of his brother; but not taking good care where he stepped, he suddenly stumbled and fell, and could not rise again until Faithful came up to help him.

Then I saw in my dream that they went very lovingly on together, and had pleasant and rewarding conversation about all the things that had happened to them in their pilgrimage.

Christian began, "My honored and well-beloved brother, Faithful, I am glad that I have overtaken you, and that God

FAITHFUL HELPS CHRISTIAN UP

has so tempered our spirits that we can walk as companions on this pleasant path.

Faithful replied, "I had thought, dear friend, to have your company quite from our town. But you got started ahead of me, and so I was forced to come this much of the way alone.

"How long did you stay in the City of Destruction before you set out after me on your pilgrimage?" asked Christian.

"Till I could stay no longer," his friend answered. "For there was great talk after you had left that our city would, in a short time, be burned down to the ground."

"What? did your neighbors talk so?"

"Yes," he replied, "it was for a while in everybody's mouth."

"But did no one other than you come out to escape the danger?" Christian asked.

Faithful shook his head. "Though there was, as I said, a great talk for a while, yet I do not think they firmly believed it. In the heat of the discourse, for instance, I heard some of them speak mockingly of you and your desperate journey (as they called your pilgrimage), but I did believe and do still that our city will end with fire and brimstone from above, and because of this I made my escape."

"Did you hear any talk of neighbor Pliable?" said Christian.

"Yes, Christian, I heard that he followed you till he came to the Slough of Despond, where, according to some reports, he fell in. But he would not let it be known that it was so, though I am sure of it, because he returned thoroughly covered with that kind of dirt."

"And what did the neighbors say to him?"

Again Faithful shook his head. "He has, since going back, been held in great derision among all sorts of people. Some mock and despise him, and hardly anyone will give him any word. He is now seven times worse off than if he had never gone out of the city."

"But why should they be so set against him?" Christian protested, "since they also despise the Way he forsook?"

Faithful replied, "Oh, they say, hang him, he is a turn-coat! He was not true to his profession. I think God has stirred up even his enemies to hiss at him and make him a proverb because he forsook the Way."[1]

Christian went on, "Had you no talk with him before you came out?"

"I met him in the streets once," replied his friend, "but he leered away on the other side, as one ashamed of what he had done. So I did not speak to him."

PLIABLE MOCKED AFTER HIS APOSTASY

"Well," said Christian, "when I set out, I had hope for that man. But now I fear he will perish with the city when it is overthrown. It has happened to him according to the true proverb, 'The dog turns back to his own vomit; and the sow is washed, only to wallow in the mire.' "[2]

"These are my fears for him, too," said Faithful. "But who can hinder that which will be?"

"Well, neighbor Faithful," said Christian, "let us leave him and talk of things that more immediately concern us. Tell me now, what have you met with in the Way as you came? For I know you have met with some things, or else it may be written as a great wonder."

"I escaped the Slough that I perceived you fell into," Faithful continued, "and got up to the gate without that danger. But then I met with one whose name was Wanton, who almost got me into real trouble."

"It was well you escaped her net," commented the other. "Joseph was hard put to it by her, and he escaped her as you did, but it almost cost him his life.[3] But what did she do to you?"

"You cannot believe what a flattering tongue she had,"

FAITHFUL AND WANTON

121

Faithful answered. "She pressed me to turn aside with her, promising me all manner of satisfaction."

"No," observed Christian, "she did *not* promise you the satisfaction of a good conscience."

"You know what I mean," replied Faithful, "all *carnal* and *fleshly* satisfaction."

"Thank God you have escaped her! 'The abhorred of the Lord shall fall into her ditch.' "[4]

"No, as a matter of fact, I do not know whether I did wholly escape her," said Faithful, shaking his head.

"What? I trust you did not consent to her desire?" exclaimed Christian.

"No, I did not defile myself, for I remembered an old writing that I had seen, 'Her steps go downward on the path to hell.'[5] So I shut my eyes, because I was determined not to be bewitched by her looks.[6] Then she railed at me, and I went on my way."

"Did you meet with any other assault as you came?" Christian inquired.

Faithful answered, "When I came to the foot of the hill called Difficulty, I met with a very aged man who asked me what I was and whither bound. I told him that I am a pilgrim, going to the Celestial City. Then said the old man, 'You look like an honest fellow. Will you content yourself to dwell with me for the wages I shall give you?' I asked his name, and where he lived. He said his name was Adam the First and that he dwelt in the town of Deceit.[7] I asked him then what was his work and what wages he would give. He told me that his work was many delights and his wages, that I should be his heir at last. I further asked him what house he kept and what other servants he had. So he told me that his house was maintained with all the dainties in the world, and that his servants were those of his own children. He said that he had three daughters, the Lust of the Flesh, the Lust of the Eyes, and the Pride of Life, and that I should marry them all if I would.[8] Then I asked how long he wanted me to live with him. He told me, as long as he lived himself.''

''Well, and what conclusion did you and the old man reach at last?'' asked Christian.

''Why, at first, I found myself somewhat inclined to go with the man, for I thought he spoke very well. But then I looked into his forehead as I talked with him, and I saw there written, ''Put off the old man with his deeds.''

''And what then?''

''Then it came burning hot into my mind, whatever he said and however he flattered, when he got me home to his house, he would sell me for a slave! So I told him to stop talking, because I would never come near the door of his house. He reviled me then, and told me that he would send one after me who would make my way bitter to my soul. So I turned to go away from him, but just as I turned, I felt him take hold of my flesh and give me such a deadly jerk back that I thought he had pulled part of me after himself. This made me cry, 'Oh, wretched man!'[9] So I went on my way up the hill.

''Now when I had gotten about halfway up, I looked behind me and saw one coming after me swift as the wind; so he overtook me just about the place where the little wayside settle stands.''

''Just there,'' said Christian, ''I sat down to rest and was overcome with sleep. It was there I lost this roll out of my bosom!''

''But, good brother, hear me out!'' exclaimed Faithful. ''As soon as the man overtook me, he was but a word and a blow, for he knocked me and laid me for dead. But when I had come to myself again, I asked him why he had treated me so, and he said it was because of my secret inclination to old Adam the First. With that he struck me another deadly blow on the breast and beat me down backward! I lay as dead as before at his feet. When I came to myself again, I cried to him for mercy, but he said, 'I know not how to show mercy!' and with that, he knocked me down again! He doubtless would have made an end of me, except that another came by and told him to forbear.''

''Who was that who told him to forbear?'' asked Christian eagerly.

''I did not know Him at first, but as He went by, I saw the holes in His hands and in His side. Then I concluded that He was our Lord. So I went up the hill.''

''That man who overtook you was Moses,'' asserted Christian. ''He spares none and does not know how to show mercy to those who transgress his law.''

''I know it very well,'' mused the other. ''It was not the first time he has met with me. It was he who came to me when I dwelt securely at home, and told me that he would burn my house over my head if I stayed there!''

''But did you not see the house that stood there on the top of the hill on which Moses met you?'' asked Christian.

''Yes,'' said Faithful, ''and I saw the lions, too, before I came to it. But I think the lions were asleep, for it was about noon. And because I had so much of the day before me, I went on down the hill.''

''The porter told me that he saw you pass,'' said Christian. ''But I wish you had called at the house, for they would have shown you many rarities that you could not forget till the day of your death. But do tell me, did you meet nobody in the Valley of Humiliation?''

''Yes, I met with one called Discontent, who would have persuaded me to go back with him if he could,'' said Faithful. ''His reason was, that the valley was altogether without honor.

He told me, moreover, that to go there would offend all my friends — Pride, Arrogancy, Self-conceit, Worldly-glory, and others he knew, as he said, who would be very much offended if I made such a fool of myself as to wade through this valley.''

''Well, and how did you answer him?'' Christian smiled as he asked the question.

FAITHFUL CUTS AND IS CUT BY HIS RELATIONS

''I told him that although all these whom he named might claim to be kin to me (and rightly so, for indeed they were my relations according to the flesh), yet since I had become a pilgrim, they had disowned me, and I also have rejected them, so they were to me now no more than if they had never been of my lineage.

"I told him moreover, that as far as this valley was concerned, he had quite misrepresented the whole thing: 'for before honor is humility, and a haughty spirit before a fall.' Therefore, said I, I had rather go through this valley to the honor that was so accounted by the wisest than choose that which he thought most worthy of our affections."

"Did you meet with anything else in that valley?" asked Christian.

"Yes," said his friend, "I met with Shame. Of all the men that I met with in my pilgrimage, I think he bears the wrong name. The others would be refused after a little argument and resistance; but this bold-faced Shame would never give up."

"Why, what did he say to you?"

"Why, he objected against religion itself!" exclaimed Faithful. "He said it was a pitiful, low, sneaking business for a man to mind religion; he said that a tender conscience was an unmanly thing, and that for a man to watch over his words and ways so as to refuse himself that unbridled liberty which the brave spirits of the time enjoy, would make a man the ridicule of the age. He objected also, that but few of the mighty, rich, or wise were ever of my opinion;[10] nor any of them,[11] either, before they were persuaded to be fools and to be of voluntary stupidity to venture the loss of everything for nobody knows what! He objected, too, to the low and despised estate and condition of those who were the majority of the pilgrims of the times in which they lived. He berated their ignorance and lack of understanding in all the natural sciences. Yes, he went on in that manner about a great many more things than I am telling here, such as, it was a *shame* to sit whining and mourning under a sermon, and a *shame* to come sighing and groaning home; that it was a *shame* to ask one's neighbor forgiveness for petty faults, or to make restitution where I have taken anything from anyone. He said that religion made a man grow estranged from the great because of their few vices (which he called by finer names), and that it made a man own and respect the base and low simply because they were of the same religious group. And is not this, he said, a *shame*?''

"And what did you say to him?" asked Christian.

"Say? I could not tell what to say at the first!" said Faithful. "He made the blood come up into my face, and I felt confused and embarrassed. But finally I began to remember that 'what is exalted among men is an abomination in the sight of God.'[12] I thought again, this Shame tells me what men are, but it tells me nothing of what God is or the Word of God is. Then I thought of Judgment Day, when we shall not be given death or life according to the swaggering and bullying spirits of the world, but according to the wisdom and law of the Most High. Therefore, thought I, what God says is best, indeed *is* best, even though everyone in the world be against it. Seeing then, that God prefers His religion; seeing that God prefers a tender conscience; seeing that they who make themselves fools for the kingdom of heaven are wisest, and that the poor man who loves Christ is richer than the greatest man in the world who hates Him — *Shame*, depart! You are an enemy of my salvation! Shall I entertain you against my sovereign Lord? How then shall I look Him in the face at His coming? Should I now be ashamed of His ways and His servants, how then can I expect the blessing?''[13]

"But this Shame was a bold villain! I could hardly shake his company. Yes, he kept on haunting me, continually whispering in my ear with some one or other of the weaknesses which attend religion. But at last I told him it was but in vain to try any further in his designs, for those things he disdained, in those I see most glory! And so, at last I got past this persistent one.''

Christian smiled at his friend. "I am glad, my brother," he said, "that you withstood this villain so bravely, for, as you say, he has the wrong name. He is so bold as to follow us in the streets and to try to put us to shame before all men — that is, to make us ashamed of all that is good. But if he was not himself so audacious, he would never attempt to do as he does. But let us resist him still, for in spite of all his bravados, he promotes the fool and no one else. 'The wise will inherit honor,' as Solomon said, 'but fools exalt disgrace.' "[14]

"I think we must cry to Him for help against this Shame," said Faithful, "Him who would have us to be valiant for the truth on the earth."

"Indeed! but did you meet no one else?" Christian still wondered about Apollyon, and whether his friend had encountered him in that dark valley.

"No," said Faithful. "I had sunshine all the way through that valley, and also through the Valley of the Shadow of Death."

"It was well that you did," Christian observed. "You can be sure it was otherwise with me. I had, for a long period, as soon as I entered into that valley, a dreadful combat with that foul fiend, Apollyon, and thought verily he was going to kill me, especially when he got me down and crushed me under him, as if he wanted to crush me to pieces. As he threw me, my sword flew out of my hand, and he told me he was sure he had me then! But I cried to God, and He heard me and delivered me out of all my troubles.

"Then I entered into the Valley of the Shadow of Death and had no light for almost halfway through it. I thought I would be killed there, over and over; but at last day broke, and the sun rose, and I went through that which was left with far more ease and quiet."

Notes on Chapter 11

[1]*Jeremiah 29:18,19* I will pursue them with sword, famine, and pestilence, and will make them a horror to all the kingdoms of the earth, to be a curse, a terror, a hissing, and a reproach among all the nations where I have driven them, because they did not heed my words, says the Lord, which I persistently sent to you by my servants the prophets, but you would not listen, says the Lord.

[2]*II Peter 2:22*

[3]*Genesis 39:11-13* for the story of Joseph and Potiphar's wife.

[4]*Proverbs 22:14*

[5]*Proverbs 5:5* (composite translation).

[6]*Job 31:1* I made a covenant with mine eyes; why then should I look upon a maid?

[7]*Ephesians 4:22* Put off your old nature which belongs to your former life and is corrupt through deceitful lusts.

[8]*I John 2:16*

[9]*Romans 7:24*

[10]*I Corinthians 1:26* For consider your call, brethren; not many of you were wise according to worldly standards, not many were powerful, nor many were of noble birth. *I Corinthians 3:18* Let no one deceive himself. If any one among you thinks that he is wise in this age, let him become a fool that he may become wise. *Phillipians 3:7,8* But whatever gain I had, I counted as loss for the sake of Christ. Indeed, I count everything as loss because of the surpassing worth of knowing Christ Jesus my Lord. For his sake I have suffered the loss of all things, and count them as refuse, in order that I may gain Christ.

[11]*John 7:48* Have any of the authorities or of the Pharisees believed in him?

[12]*Luke 16:15*

[13]*Mark 8:38* For whoever is ashamed of me and of my words in this adulterous and sinful generation, of him will the Son of Man also be ashamed, when he comes in the glory of his Father with the holy angels.

[14]*Proverbs 3:35*

Talkative Joins the Pilgrims

I saw in my dream that as they went on, Faithful noticed a man walking at some distance beside them on the road, for in this place there was room enough for all of them to walk. He was a tall man, somewhat more attractive at a distance than close at hand. To this man Faithful spoke in this manner:

"Friend, where are you going? Are you on your way to the heavenly country?"

"Yes," replied the man, "I am going to the same place."

"Well, then I hope we may have your good company."

"With a very good will I will walk with you," replied the stranger.

"Come on then," said Faithful, "and let us get on together, and spend our time talking of profitable things."

"It is very acceptable to me to talk of good things with you or with any other," said the newcomer. "I am glad that I have met with those who incline to such a good work, because, to be truthful, there are few who care to spend their time in such a way. Most people, I find, would rather spend their time speaking of things that really don't matter, and this bothers me.''

"That is indeed a thing to be lamented,'' commented Faithful. "What things are so worthy of the use of the tongue and mouth of men on earth as the things of God in heaven?''

"I like you wonderfully well,'' the newcomer went on. "Your sayings are full of conviction. I will add, what thing is so pleasant and what so profitable as to talk of the things of God? What things are so pleasant, that is, if a man has any delight in things that are wonderful? For instance, if a man delights to talk of history or the mystery of things, or if a man loves to talk of miracles, wonders or signs, where shall he find things written that are as delightful and sweetly written as in the Holy Scriptures?''

"That is true,'' said Faithful. "But our aim should be to be benefited by such things in our talk.''

"That's what I said,'' the other retorted. "For to talk of such things is profitable. By so doing, a man may get knowledge of many things, such as the vanity of earthly things and the benefit of things above. Thus, in general, but more particularly, by doing this, a man may learn the necessity of the new birth, the insufficiency of our works, the need of Christ's righteousness, and so on and so on. Besides, by this, a man may learn, by talking, what it is to repent, to pray, to suffer and the like. By this also a man may learn what are the great promises and consolations of the gospel, to his own comfort. Furthermore, by talking, a man may learn to refute false opinions, to vindicate the truth and to instruct the ignorant!''

Faithful hesitated a little before remarking, "All this is true, and I am glad to hear these things from you.''

Talkative hurried on: "Alas! the lack of this is the cause that so few understand the need of faith, and the necessity of a work of grace in their soul in order to attain eternal life. Instead, they ignorantly live in the works of the law, by which man can by no means obtain the kingdom of heaven.''

"But, with your permission," Faithful interjected, "heavenly knowledge of these things is the gift of God. No man can get it by human effort or only by talking of them.''

"All this I know very well," said the other, "for a man can receive nothing except it be given him from heaven. All is of grace, not of works. I could give you a hundred scriptures for confirming this!''

"Well then," said Faithful, "what is that one thing that we shall at this time base our discourse upon?''

"What you will," said Talkative. "I will talk of things heavenly or things earthly; things moral or things evangelical; things sacred or things profane; things past or things to come; things foreign or things at home; things more essential or things circumstantial; provided that it all be done to our profit.''

Now Faithful began to wonder, and stepping to Christian (for he was walking all this time alone), he said to him, softly, "What a brave companion we have here! Surely this man will make a very excellent pilgrim.''

At this Christian modestly smiled and said, "This man, with whom you are so taken, will beguile with that tongue of his twenty people who don't know him!''

"Do you know him then?" asked Faithful.

"Know him!" exclaimed Christian. "I know him better than he knows himself!''

"What is he, then?" Faithful asked, glancing at Talkative.

"His name is Talkative," said Christian. "He lives in our town, and I am surprised that you don't know him, though I realize that our town is a large one.''

"Whose son is he? And where does he live?" inquired Faithful.

"He is the son of one Say-well; he lived in Prating Row, and he is known to all that are acquainted with him by the name of Talkative of Prating Row. Notwithstanding his fine tongue, he is but a sorry fellow."

"Well, he seems to be a very clever man," Faithful rejoined.

Christian replied, "Yes, to those who have no thorough knowledge of him. He is best abroad, because near home he is known to be ugly enough. Your saying that he is a clever man brings to my mind what I have observed in the work of the painter, whose pictures show best at a distance, but close up are less pleasing!"

TALKATIVE AT THE ALEHOUSE

TALKATIVE AT HOME

"But I almost think you are jesting, because you smiled," his friend continued.

"God forbid that I should jest in this matter even though I smiled," Christian exclaimed. "And God forbid that I should accuse anyone falsely! I will tell you this, too, about him. This man is for any company and for any talk. As he talks now with you, so will he talk when he is on the ale-bench; and the more drink he has in his head, the more of those things he has in his mouth; religion has no place in his heart or home, nor in his manner of life. All he has lies in his tongue, and his religion is, to make a noise with it."

"Is that so!" said Faithful emphatically. "Then I am greatly deceived in this man."

"Deceived? You may be sure of it. Remember the proverb, 'They say and do not.'[1] But the 'kingdom of God is not in word, but in power.'[2] This man talks of prayer, of repentance, of faith, and of the new birth; but he knows only to talk of them. I have been in his family and have observed him both at home and abroad, and I know that what I say of him is the truth. His home is as empty of faith in God as the white of an egg is of taste. There is there neither prayer, nor any sign of repentance for sin — yes, the dumb animals in their own way serve God far better than he. He is the very stain, reproach, and shame of all religion to all who know him. There is hardly a good word to be said about him in all that end of town where he lives.[3] The common people who know him say of him, 'A saint abroad, and a devil at home.' His poor family finds it so. He is such a rude and boorish man, such a railer at and so unreasonable with his servants, that they neither know how to do for him nor how to speak to him. Men who have any dealings with him say it is better to deal with an outlaw than with him, for they will get fairer dealings than from him. This Talkative will go beyond what an outlaw would do in order to defraud, beguile and outwit them. In addition to this, he brings up his sons to follow his steps, and if he finds in any of them a foolish timidity (for that is what he terms even the first appearance of a tender conscience), he calls them fools and blockheads, and will not employ them himself, nor recommend them to anyone else. For my part, I am of the opinion that he has, by his wicked life, caused many to stumble and fall, and will be the ruin of many more, if God does not prevent it."

"Well, my brother," said Faithful gravely, "I am bound to believe you; not only because you say you know him, but because you have always, as a Christian should, spoken only the truth concerning others. I cannot think that you speak these things out of any ill-will, but because it is just as you say."

"Had I not known him any more than you, I might perhaps have thought of him as you did at first," continued Christian. "And if he had been characterized in this way only by those who are enemies to religion, I would have considered it a slander — a lot that often falls from bad men's mouths upon good men's names and professions! But all these things, yea, and a great many more equally bad I could prove him to be guilty of to my own knowledge. And besides, good men are ashamed of him. They can neither call him brother nor friend! The very mention of his name among them makes them blush if they know him."

"Well," commented Faithful, "I see that saying and doing are two different things, and hereafter, I should better observe this distinction!"

"They are two things, indeed," said his friend. "They are as diverse as the soul and body; for as the body without the soul is but a dead carcass, so talking, if it is alone, is but a dead carcass, too. The soul of religion is the practical part: 'Pure religion and undefiled before God and the Father is this, to visit the fatherless and widows in their affliction, and to keep himself unspotted from the world.'[4] Talkative is not aware of this. He thinks that hearing and saying will make a good Christian, and thus he deceives his own soul. Hearing is but as the sowing of the seed. Talking is not sufficient to prove that fruit is indeed in the heart and life. Let us assure ourselves that at the day of judgment men shall be judged according to their fruits.[5] It will not be said to them then, 'Did you believe?' but rather, 'Were you doers, or talkers only?' And accordingly they shall be judged. The end of the world is compared to our harvest; and you know men at harvest regard nothing but fruit. Not that anything can be accepted that is not of faith, but I speak this to show you how insignificant the profession of Talkative will be in that day."

"That brings to my mind a word of Moses, by which he

describes the animal that is clean," said Faithful.[6] "A clean animal is one that parts the hoof and chews the cud — not that parts the hoof only, or chews the cud only. The rabbit chews the cud, but yet is unclean, because he does not part the hoof. And this truly resembles this Talkative. He chews the cud, he seeks knowledge, he chews on the word, but he does not divide the hoof — he does not part with the way of sinners. Instead, as the hare, he retains the foot of a dog or bear, and therefore he is unclean."

Christian said, "You have spoken, as far as I can see, the true gospel-sense of those texts. I will add another thing: Paul calls some men — yes, and those were great talkers, too — 'sounding brass and tinkling cymbals.' That means, as he explains in another place, 'things without life, giving sound.'[7] Things without life — that is, without the true faith and grace of the gospel, and consequently, things that shall never be placed in the kingdom of heaven among those who are the children of life; though by their sound, by their talk, appear as though it were the tongue of an angel!"

"Well, I was not so fond of his company at first, but I am as sick of it now," said Faithful emphatically. "But what shall we do to get rid of him?"

"Take my advice, and do as I tell you, and you shall find that *he* will soon be sick of your company, too, unless God touches his heart and turns it," advised the other.

"What would you have me to do?"

"Why, go to him, and enter into some serious discourse about the power of religion," said Christian. "Ask him plainly, when he has approved of it (for he will do that!), whether or not this thing is set up in his heart, his home and his way of life."

Then Faithful stepped forward again, and said to Talkative, "Come, what cheer? How is it now?"

"Thank you, well," replied Talkative. "I thought we should have had a great deal of talk by this time."

"Well, if you like, we will have it now," replied Faithful. "And since you left it with me to state the question, let it be this: how does the saving grace of God reveal itself, when it is in the heart of a man?"

"I perceive then that our talk must be about the power of things," Talkative bubbled. "Well, it is a very good question, and I shall be willing to answer you. And take my answer in brief, thus: First, where the grace of God is in the heart, it causes a great outcry there against sin. Secondly —"

"Wait!" cried Faithful, "hold on! Let's consider one at a time. I think you should rather say, it shows itself by inclining the soul to abhor *its* sin."

Talkative looked puzzled. "Why, what difference is there between crying out against sin, and abhorring sin?"

"Oh, a great deal," Faithful continued. "A man may cry out against sin because it is considered a good policy to do so. But he cannot abhor sin except by a holy hatred of it. I have heard many cry out against sin in the pulpit who can yet abide it well enough in the heart, the home, and in their manner of life. Joseph's master's wife cried out with a loud voice, as if she had been very holy; but she would willingly, notwithstanding her crying out, have committed adultery with him.[8] Some people cry out against sin even as a mother cries out against her child in her lap, when she calls it a brat or a slut, and then falls to hugging and kissing it."

"I perceive that you set traps in your talk," Talkative rejoined petulantly.

"No, not I," answered Faithful. "I am only for setting things right. But what is the second thing whereby you would prove a discovery of a work of God's grace in the heart?"

"Great knowledge of gospel mysteries," answered

Talkative.

Faithful said, "This sign should have been mentioned first; but first or last, it is also false. For knowledge, great knowledge, may be obtained in the mysteries of the gospel, and yet there be no work of grace in the soul.[9] Yes, if a man have all knowledge, he may yet be nothing, and so consequently he is not a child of God. When Christ said, 'Do you know all these things?' and the disciples answered, 'Yes,' he added, 'Blessed are you if you do them.' He does not lay the blessing in the knowing, but in the doing of them. For there is a knowledge that is not accompanied by doing: 'He that knows his master's will, and does it not.' A man may know like an angel, and yet be no Christian. Therefore, your sign of great knowledge of gospel mysteries is not a true one. Indeed, to *know* is a thing that pleases talkers and boasters. But to *do* is what pleases God. Not that the heart can be good without knowledge; for without that, the heart is naught. There is, therefore, knowledge and knowledge. Knowledge that rests in the bare speculation of things, and knowledge that is accompanied with the grace of faith and love, which sets a man to doing the will of God from his heart. The first of these will serve the talker, but without the other, the true Christian is not content. 'Give me understanding, and I shall keep thy law; yea, I shall observe it with my whole heart.' "[10]

Talkative responded, "Setting the trap again with your words, I see. This is not edifying or profitable."

"Well, if you please, propound another sign how this work of grace reveals its presence in a man's heart," offered Faithful.

"Not I," said Talkative, "for I see we shall not agree."

"Well, if you will not, will you permit me to do it?" asked Faithful.

"You are free to do as you wish," said Talkative sullenly.

Faithful continued: ''A work of grace in the soul reveals itself, either to him who has it, or to those who know him.

''To the person who has such a work, this is what it does: it gives him conviction of sin, especially of the defilement of his nature and the sin of unbelief. He knows that he will be condemned for his unbelief if he does not find mercy at God's hand by faith in Jesus Christ.[11] This sight and sense of things works in him both sorrow and shame for sin. He finds, moreover, revealed in Him the Savior of the world, and the absolute necessity of closing with Him for life.[12] He finds himself hungering and thirsting for Him, and finds it is to those who hunger and thirst for righteousness that the promise has been made.[13] Now, according to the strength or weakness of his faith in his Savior, so is his joy and peace, so is his love for holiness, so are his desires to know Him more, and to serve Him in this world. But though I say it discloses itself in this way to the person who has a work of grace going on within him, because of his corruptions, his abused reason, and his past experiences, he may indeed misjudge this matter, and it is important, therefore that a man have a very sound judgment before he can dare conclude that this is indeed a work of grace.

''To those who know the person, the work of grace reveals itself in these ways:

''First, by an experimental confession of his faith in Christ.[14]

''Secondly, by a life consistent with that confession. By that I mean a life of holiness, heart-holiness, family-holiness (if he has a family), and by holiness in his manner of living in the world. Inwardly, he abhors his sin and himself because of it, in secret. Then he seeks to suppress sin in his family, and to promote holiness in the world — not by talk only, as a hypocrite or talkative person may do, but by a practical subjection, in faith and love, to the power of the Word.[15] Now sir, as to this brief description of the work of grace and how it discloses itself, if you have any objection, by all means, speak it. If not, then will you permit me to propound a second question to you?''

Talkative said somewhat quietly, "No, my part is not now to object, but to hear. So let me have your second question."

"It is this," replied Faithful. "Do you experience the first part of my description of the work of grace, and do your life and your way of living testify the same? Or does your religion stand in word or in tongue, and not in deed and in truth. If you incline to answer me in this, say no more than you know God above will say Amen to; and say nothing but what your conscience can justify you in; 'for, it is not the man who commends himself that is accepted, but the man whom the Lord commends.'[16] Besides, to say I am so and so, when my life and all my neighbors tell me that I am lying, is indeed great wickedness.''

Then Talkative at first began to blush, but recovering himself, he replied, "You come now to experience, to conscience and God; and to appeal to him for justification of what is spoken. This kind of talk I did not expect, nor am I disposed to give an answer to such questions, because I do not count myself bound to, unless you take upon yourself to be a catechizer. Even then, I may yet refuse to make you my judge! But, may I ask, why you ask me such questions?''

Faithful answered, "Because I saw that you were quick to talk, and because I did not know whether you had anything but notions and opinions. Besides, to tell you all the truth, I have heard of you, that you are a man whose religion lies in your talk, and that your way of life gives this mouth-profession of yours the lie. They say that other Christians do not welcome you, and that the whole cause of religion suffers because of your ungodly life, that some have already stumbled at your wicked ways, and that more are in danger of being destroyed by them. Your religion, an ale-house, and covetousness, and uncleanness, and swearing and lying, and keeping vain company (to name a few) — all stand together. The proverb is true of you which is said of a whore, namely, that she is a shame to all women. So are you a shame to all who profess faith in Christ!''

"Since you are ready to take up reports and to judge so rashly as you do," said Talkative angrily, "I cannot but conclude you are some peevish or melancholy man, not fit to be talked with in any serious way. And so, I bid you good-bye."

Then Christian caught up with his brother and said, "I told you how it would happen. Your words and his lusts could not agree; he would rather leave your company than reform his life. But he is gone, as I said. Let him go — the loss is no man's but his own. He has saved us the trouble of leaving him ourselves, for if he continues to go on as he is (as I suppose he will do), he would have been a blot in our company. The apostle says, 'From such turn away.' ''17

"But I am glad we had this little discourse with him," replied Faithful. "It may happen that he will think of it again. However, I have dealt plainly with him, and so am clear of his blood, if he perishes."

Christian answered, "You did well to talk as plainly with him as you did. There is but little of this faithful dealing with men now-a-days, and that makes our faith to stink in the nostrils of many, so that they underestimate its worth. When these talkative fools whose religion is only in word, who are so debauched and empty in their walk in the world are even admitted into fellowship of the godly, it is a puzzlement to the world, a blemish to Christianity, and a grief to the sincere. I wish that all Christians would deal with such people as you have done: Then should their lives either be made more consistent with the faith they say they have, or the company of the faithful would be too hot for them."

They went on talking in this way of what they had seen along their pilgrimage, and so made that part of the Way easy which otherwise would have doubtless been tedious to them. For they were now going through a desert-like place.

Notes on Chapter 12

[1]*Matthew 23:3*

[2]*I Corinthians 4:20*

[3]*Romans 2:24* For as it is written, "The name of God is blasphemed among the Gentiles because of you."

[4]*James 1:27 (see also vss. 23-26)*

[5]*Matthew 13:23* As for what was sown on good soil, this is he who hears the word and understands it; he indeed bears fruit and yields, in one case a hundredfold, in another sixty, and in another, thirty.

[6]*Leviticus 11:3* Whatever parts the hoof and is cloven-footed and chews the cud, among the animals, you may eat. *Deuteronomy 14:6* Every animal that parts the hoof and has the hoof cloven in two, and chews the cud, among the animals, you may eat. Yet of those that chew the cud or have the hoof cloven you shall not eat these: the camel, the hare, and the rock badger, because they chew the cud but do not part the hoof, are unclean for you.

[7]*I Corinthians 13:1-3* If I speak in the tongues of men and of angels, but have not love, I am a noisy gong or a clanging cymbal. And if I have prophetic powers, and understand all mysteries and all knowledge, and if I have all faith, so as to remove mountains, and have not love, I am nothing. If I give away all I have, and if I deliver my body to be burned, but have not love, I gain nothing. *I Corinthians 14:7* If even lifeless instruments, such as the flute or harp, do not give distinct notes, how will anyone know what is played?

[8]*Genesis 39:15*

[9]*I Corinthians 13*

[10]*Psalm 119:34*

[11]*John 16:8* And when he (the Counselor) comes, he will convince the world of sin and of righteousness and of judgment. *Romans 7:24* Wretched man that I am! Who will deliver me from this body of death? *John 16:9* Of sin, because they do not believe in me... *Mark 16:16* He who believes and is baptized will be saved; but he who does not believe will be condemned.

[12]I have left Bunyan's original expression here, which means to accept Jesus as Lord and Savior, to *close* or complete the transaction. " 'Tis done! The great transaction's done! I am the Lord's and He is mine!" (Philip Doddridge)

[13]*Psalm 38:18* I confess my iniquity, I am sorry for my sin. *Jeremiah 31:19* For after I had turned away I repented; and after I was instructed, I smote upon my thigh; I was ashamed, and I was confounded, because I bore the disgrace of my youth. *Galatians 2:16* Yet who know that a man is not justified by works of the law but through faith in Jesus Christ, even we have believed in Christ Jesus, in order to be justified by faith in Christ, and not by works of the law, because by works of the law shall no one be justified. *Acts 4:12* And there is salvation in no one else, for there is no other name under heaven given among men by which we must be saved. *Matthew 5:6* Blessed are those who hunger and thirst for righteousness, for they shall be satisfied. *Revelation 21:6* And he said to me, "It is done! I am the Alpha and the Omega, the beginning and the end. To the thirsty I will give water without price from the fountain of the water of life."

[14]*Romans 10:10* For man believes with his heart and so is justified, and he confesses with his lips and so is saved. *Phillipians 1:27* Only let your manner of life be worthy of the gospel of Christ, so that whether I come and see you or am absent, I may hear of you that you stand firm in one spirit, with one mind striving side by side for the faith of the gospel. *Matthew 5:19* Whoever then relaxes one of the least of these commandments and teaches men so, shall be called least in the kingdom of heaven; but he who does them and teaches them shall be called great in the kingdom of heaven.

Our author here weights down his narrative with these Scripture references, because of their vital importance to anyone who may be reading his book. These are the simple, basic truths by which we are to be convicted of our sin and our need for salvation in none other than our Lord Jesus Christ. *Ed.*

[15]*John 14:15* If you love me, you will keep my commandments. *Psalm 1:2* But his delight is in the law of the Lord, and on his law he meditates day and night. *Psalm 50:23* He who brings thanksgiving as his sacrifice honors me; to him who orders his way aright I will show the salvation of God. *Job 42:5,6* I had heard of thee by the hearing of the ear, but now my eye seeth thee; therefore I despise myself and repent in dust and ashes. *Ezekiel 20:43* And there you shall remember your ways and all the doings with which you have polluted yourselves; and you shall loathe yourselves for all the evils that you have committed.

[16]*II Corinthians 10:18*

[17]*II Timothy 3:5*

13

Christian and Faithful at Vanity Fair

When they were almost out of this wilderness, Faithful chanced to look back, and saw one coming after them whom they both knew.

"Oh!" said Faithful to his brother. "Who comes yonder?"

Christian looked back and said, "It is my good friend, Evangelist."

"Yes, and my good friend, too," said Faithful, "for it was he who set me on the way to the gate."

Evangelist soon overtook them, and coming up greeted them, "Peace be with you, dearly beloved; and peace be to your helpers."

"Welcome, welcome, good Evangelist," said Christian heartily. "The sight of your face brings to my remembrance your former kindness and your unwearied labor for my eternal good."

"And a thousand times welcome," said good Faithful. "Your company, O sweet Evangelist, — how desirable it is to us poor Pilgrims!"

Then said Evangelist, "How has it fared with you, my

friends, since the time of our last parting? What have you met with, and how have you behaved yourselves?''

Christian and Faithful then told him of all the things that had happened to them in the Way, and how they had arrived where they were and what difficulties they had met.

''I am glad indeed,'' said Evangelist, ''not that you have met with trials, but that you have been victors. For that's what you have been — victors — in spite of your many weaknesses, because you have continued in this Way to this very day.

''I say that I am glad of this thing, and glad for my sake as well as yours. I have sowed, and you have reaped. The day is coming when both he who sowed and he who reaped shall rejoice together — that is, if you hold out. 'For in due season you shall reap, if you faint not.'[1] 'The crown is before you, and it is an incorruptible one; so run that you may obtain it.'[2] There are some who set out for this crown, and after they have gone far for it, someone else comes in and takes it from them. Hold fast, therefore, what you have. Let no man take your crown.[3] You are not yet out of gun-shot of the devil. You have not yet resisted unto blood, striving against sin. Let the kingdom be always before you, and believe steadfastly concerning things that are invisible. Let nothing that is on this side of the world to come get within you; and above all, look well to your own hearts and to the lusts of them, 'for they are deceitful above all things, and desperately wicked.' Set your faces like a flint. You have all power in heaven and earth on your side.''

Then Christian thanked him for his exhortation, but told him that they would have him speak further to them, to help them the rest of the way. They knew well, Christian said, that he was a prophet and could tell them of things that might happen to them and how they might resist and overcome them. Faithful, too, joined in asking Evangelist to speak further.

So Evangelist continued his discourse.

"My sons, you have heard, in the words of the truth of the gospel, that you must, through many tribulations enter the kingdom of heaven. Again, that in every city bonds and afflictions await you, and that you cannot expect that you should go long on your pilgrimage without them in some way or another. You have already found something of the truth of these testimonies, and more will soon follow. For now, you see, you are almost out of this wilderness, and therefore you will soon come into a town that you will soon see before you; and in that town you will be hardly beset with enemies, who will strain hard to kill you. Be sure that one or both of you must seal the testimony which you hold with blood. But be faithful unto death, and the King will give you a crown of life. He who shall die there, although his death will be unnatural, and his pain perhaps great — will yet have the better of his fellow — not only because he will arrive at the Celestial City sooner, but because he will escape many miseries that the other will meet with in the rest of his journey. But when you have come to the town and shall find fulfilled what I have related, then remember your friend, and quit yourselves like men, and commit the keeping of your souls to your God in well-doing, as unto a faithful Creator."

I saw then in my dream that when they had gotten out of the wilderness, they presently saw a town before them. The name of the town is Vanity, and in that town there is held a fair, known as Vanity Fair. It is kept all the year long. It is called Vanity Fair because the town where it is kept is lighter than vanity;[4] also, because all that is sold or comes from the town is vanity. As is the saying of the wise, "All that cometh is vanity."[5]

This fair is not newly built, but is a thing of ancient standing. I will show you how it began.

About five thousand years ago, there were pilgrims walking

to the Celestial City as Christian and Faithful were presently walking. Beelzebub, Apollyon and Legion, with their companions, perceiving by the path that the pilgrims made their way to the city lay through this town of Vanity, contrived to set up a fair there. It was a fair in which all sorts of vanity

VANITY FAIR

should be sold, and would last all the year long. Therefore at this fair all kinds of things are sold, such as houses, lands, trades, professions, places, honors, preferments, titles, countries, kingdoms, lusts, pleasures and delights of all sorts, — such as prostitutes, wives, husbands, children, masters, servants, lives, blood, bodies, souls, silver, gold, pearls, precious stones and what not.

Moreover, at this fair there is at all times to be seen juggling, cheats, games, plays, fools, mimics, knaves, and rogues of every kind. Here are to be seen, too (and that for nothing), thefts, murders, adulteries, false swearers, and obscenities of all kinds.

As in other fairs of less importance, there are several rows and streets, under their proper names, where various wares are sold. So here likewise you have the proper places, rows, streets (namely, countries and kingdoms), where the wares of this fair are most easily found. Here is the British Row, the French Row, the Italian Row, the Spanish Row, the German Row, where several sorts of vanities are to be sold.

Now, as I said, the way to the Celestial City lies just through this town where this fair is kept. He who would go to the City without going through this town would indeed need to go out of the world.[6] The Prince of princes himself, when here, went through this town to His own country, and that upon a fair day, too. Yes, and I think it was Beelzebub, the chief lord of this fair, who invited Him to buy of his vanities. He would have made Him lord of the fair if He had but done him reverence as He went through the town.[7] Because He was such a person of honor, Beelzebub had Him from street to street, and showed Him all the kingdoms of the world in a little time, so that he might, if possible, allure the Blessed One to cheapen and buy some of his vanities. But He had no mind to buy any of his merchandise, and therefore left the town without laying out so much as one red cent upon these vanities.

This fair, therefore, is an ancient thing, of long standing, and a very great fair. Now these Pilgrims, as I said, had to go through it. Well, so they did; but even as they entered the fair, their presence caused a stir among the people and the town was in a hubbub about them. This was caused by several things. First, the Pilgrims were clothed with a different kind of clothing from that bought and sold at the fair. The people of the fair, therefore, gazed at them, and some said they were fools, others thought they were crazy, some simply called them outlandish.[8]

Secondly, the people were not only offended by their clothing, but by their speech as well. Few could understand what they said. The Pilgrims naturally spoke the language of Canaan, but those who kept the fair were men of this world, so that from one end of the fair to the other, the Pilgrims and the men of the fair seemed barbarians each to the other.

Thirdly, what offended the men of the fair most was that the Pilgrims took little interest in their goods, and did not care so much as to look on them. If they were called on to buy, the Pilgrims would put their fingers in their ears, crying, "Turn away my eyes from seeing vanity," and they would look upwards, signifying that their trade and traffic was in heaven.[9]

One chanced mockingly, seeing the way the Pilgrims carried themselves, to say to them, "What will you buy?" They in turn looked very seriously at him and answered, "We buy the truth."[10] At that the townsmen took offense and began to make sport of the Pilgrims — some mocking, some taunting, some speaking reproachfully, and some calling upon others to smite them. Finally things came to such a hubbub and stirring in the fair that everything was in disorder. At this point the great one at the fair was given word about the Pilgrims' presence and all the confusion. He came down quickly and authorized some of his most trusted friends to take these men in to be examined, since they were turning the fair upside down. So

the men were brought to examination. Their examiners asked
them where they came from and what they were doing there in
such unusual garb. The men told them that they were going
to their own country, which was the heavenly Jerusalem.[11]
They said they had given no occasion to the men of the town,
nor to the merchandisers to abuse them in this manner or to
hinder them on their way; unless it could be that, when one
asked them what they would buy, they said they would buy the
truth. But those who were appointed to examine them did not
believe them to be any but lunatics or madmen, or else such as
come to put all things into confusion in a fair. Therefore they
took them and beat them, and smeared them with dirt, and
then put them into a cage so that they might be made a spectacle to all the men of Vanity Fair.

THE PILGRIMS IN THE CAGE

There they lay for some time, and were made the object of sport, malice, or revenge — the great one of the fair still laughing at all that befell them. But the men were patient, and did not return railing for railing. On the other hand, when cursed, they blessed, and gave good words for bad, kindness for injuries done. Some men in the fair who were more observant and less prejudiced than their fellows, began to stop what they were doing, and to blame the baser sort for their continual abuses to the Pilgrims. But this resulted only in stirring up the anger of the mob against them as well, so that they were counted as bad as the Pilgrims in the cage, and were called confederates and that they should be sharers in their misfortunes. The others replied that as far as they could see, these Pilgrims were quiet and sober, and intended nobody any harm. They said moreover that there were many who traded in the fair who were more deserving of being put into the cage — yes, even the pillory — than were these men who had been so abused. After many words had passed on both sides, they fell to blows among themselves, and did harm one to another. The two Christians had behaved themselves wisely and soberly during all this, but they were again brought before their examiners and charged as being guilty of the near-riot that had been in the fair. So they beat them pitifully, and hanged iron cuffs and chains on them and led them up and down the fair, as an example and a terror to others, lest any should speak in their behalf or join themselves to them. Christian and Faithful behaved themselves yet more wisely, and received the ignominy and shame which was cast upon them with so much meekness and patience that it won to their side several of the men in the fair, though these were but few in comparison with the rest. But this put the other party into an even greater rage, insomuch that they concluded that these two men should be put to death. They threatened that neither the cage nor the irons

CHRISTIAN AND FAITHFUL LED IN CHAINS UP AND DOWN THE FAIR

would do, but that they should die for the abuse they had done, and for deluding the men of the fair.

Then they were put back into the cage again until further plans could be made, and this time, their feet were put in the stocks as well.

Christian and Faithful called to mind again what they had heard from their faithful friend Evangelist, and were the more confirmed in their way and in their sufferings by what he told them would happen to them. They comforted each other, remembering that he whose lot it was to suffer, would have the best of it. Therefore each man secretly wished that he might have that preferment; but committing themselves to the all-wise disposal of Him who rules all things, with much content they remained in the condition in which they found themselves until they should be otherwise disposed of.

At the appointed time, they were brought forth to their trial in order to be condemned. The trial judge's name was Lord Hate-good. Their indictment was one and the same in sub-

LORD HATEGOOD

stance, though they varied somewhat in form. The contents of their indictment were as follows:

"That they were enemies to and disturbers of their trade; that they had made commotions and divisions in the town, and had won a party to their own most dangerous opinions, in contempt of the law of their prince."

Faithful began to answer that he had only set himself against that which had set itself against Him who is higher than the highest. "And," said he, "as for disturbance, I make none, being myself a man of peace. The parties that were won to us were won by beholding our truth and innocence, and they have only turned from the worse to the better. And as to the king you talk of, since he is Beelzebub, the enemy of our Lord, I defy him and all his angels."

Then proclamation was made, that if any had aught to say for their lord the king against the prisoner at the bar, they should forthwith appear and give their evidence. So there came in three witnesses — Envy, Superstition and Sycophant.[12] They were then asked if they knew the prisoner at the bar, and what they had to say for their lord the king against him.

Envy stood forth and spoke thus: "My Lord, I have known this man for a long time, and will attest upon my oath before this honorable bench that he is — "

"Hold!" cried the Judge. "Give him his oath!"

So they swore him in, and he continued, "My Lord, this man, notwithstanding his plausible name, is one of the vilest men in our country. He neither regards prince nor people, law nor custom, but does all that he can to possess all men with certain of his disloyal notions, which he in general calls principles of faith and holiness. In particular I heard him once myself affirm that Christianity and the customs of our town of Vanity were diametrically opposite and could not be reconciled. By this saying, my Lord, he at once condemns all our laudable doings and ourselves as well who do them."

Then the Judge said to Envy, "Have you any more to say?"

"My Lord," he replied, "I could say much more, only I would not wish to be tedious to the court. Yet, if need be, when the other gentlemen have given in their evidence, rather than that anything should be lacking to dispatch this man, I will gladly enlarge my testimony against him." So he was bidden to stand by.

They then called Superstition, and bid him look upon the prisoner, and asked what he could say for their lord the king against this man. Having been sworn in, he began.

"My Lord, I have no great acquaintance with this man, nor do I desire to have further knowledge of him. However, this I know: that he is a very pestilent fellow, from some of the discourse that I had with him the other day in this town. I heard him say as I was talking with him that our religion was nothing and that it is such by which a man can by no means please God. Your Lordship knows very well what will follow from such talk as this — that we worship in vain and are yet in our sins, and finally shall be damned. And this is what I have to say against him."

Sycophant was then sworn, and bidden to say what he knew, in behalf of their lord the king against the prisoner at the bar.

"My Lord, and you gentlemen all," Sycophant began, "this fellow I have known of a long time, and I have heard him speak things that ought not to be spoke. For he has railed on our noble prince, Beelzebub, and has spoken contemptuously of his honorable friends, the Lord Old Man, the Lord Carnal Delight, the Lord Luxurious, the Lord Desire of Vain Glory, my old Lord Lechery, Sir Having Greedy, with all the rest of our nobility; and moreover, this man has said that if all men were of his mind, not one of these noblemen would be allowed to live any longer in this town. Besides this, he has not been afraid to rail on you, my Lord, who are now appointed to be his judge, calling you an ungodly villain, and many other such vilifying terms with which he has spattered most of the gentry of our town.''

When this Sycophant had told his tale, the Judge directed his speech to the prisoner at the bar, saying, ''You renegade, heretic and traitor! Have you heard what these honest gentlemen have witnessed against you?''

''May I speak a few words in my own defense?'' asked Faithful.

FAITHFUL SPEAKS IN HIS OWN DEFENSE.

"Scum!" cried the Judge. "You don't deserve to live any longer, and ought to be slain immediately right here! But, so that all men may see our gentleness towards you, let us hear what you, vile reprobate that you are, have to say!"

Faithful spoke. "I say, then, in answer to what Mr. Envy has said, that I never said anything but this, that any rule or law or custom or people that were flatly against the Word of God are diametrically opposed to Christianity. If I have spoken amiss in this, convince me of my error and I am ready here before you to make my recantation.

"Secondly, as to Mr. Superstition's charge against me, I said only this, that in the worship of God there is required a Divine faith; but there can be no Divine faith without a Divine revelation of the will of God. Therefore, whatever is thrust into the worship of God that is not agreeable to Divine revelation cannot be done by anything other than by a human faith, which will not be profitable to eternal life.

"As to what Mr. Sycophant said, I say (avoiding terms such as that I am said to rail, and the like) that the prince of this town with all the rabblement, his attendants whom this gentleman named, are more fit for living in hell than in this town and country. And so, the Lord have mercy upon me!"

The Judge then called the jury, who all this while stood by to hear and to observe.

"Gentlemen of the jury," he said, "you see this man about whom so great an uproar has been made in this town. You have also heard his reply and confession. It lies now in your breasts to hang him or save his life; but yet I think it proper to instruct you in our law.

"There was an Act made in the days of Pharaoh the Great, servant to our prince, that, lest those of a contrary religion should multiply and grow too strong for him, their males should be thrown into the river.[13] There was also an Act made in the days of Nebuchadnezzar the Great, another of his servants, that whosoever would not fall down and worship his golden image should be cast into a fiery furnace.[14] There was also an Act made in the days of Darius, that whoever for a time, called upon any god but him, should be thrown into the lions' den.[15] Now the substance of these laws this rebel has broken, not only in thought (which cannot be allowed) but also in word and deed. This is absolutely intolerable!

"For the law of Pharaoh was made upon a supposition that it would prevent mischief, since no crime was yet apparent. But here is a crime apparent. For the second and third, you see he disputes against our religion. For the treason he has confessed, he deserves to die the death."

Then the jury went out. Their names were Mr. Blind-man, Mr. No-good, Mr. Malice, Mr. Love-lust, Mr. Live-loose, Mr. Heady, Mr. High-mind, Mr. Enmity, Mr. Liar, Mr. Cruelty, Mr. Hate-light and Mr. Implacable. Every one of them handed in his private verdict against him among themselves, and afterwards they unanimously concluded to bring in a verdict of guilty before the Judge. First, among themselves, Mr. Blind-man, the foreman, said, "I see clearly that this man is a heretic." Then said Mr. No-good, "Away with such a fellow from the earth." "Aye," said Mr. Malice, "for I hate the very looks of him."

Then Mr. Love-lust said, "I could never endure him." "Nor I," said Mr. Live-loose, "for he would always be condemning my way."

"Hang him, hang him," said Mr. Heady. "A sorry scrub," said Mr. High-mind.

"My heart rises against him," said Mr. Enmity. "He is a rogue," said Mr. Liar. "Hanging is too good for him," said Mr. Cruelty. "Let us dispatch him out of the way," said Mr. Hate-light. Then said Mr. Implacable, "For all the world

THE JURY AGREE IN THEIR VERDICT.

I could not be reconciled to him. Therefore let us declare him guilty of death."

And so they did. Presently he was condemned to be taken from the place where he was, back to the place from whence he came, and there to be put to the most cruel death that could be invented.

They brought him out to do with him according to their law. First, they scourged him, then they buffeted him, then they lanced his flesh with knives. After that, they stoned him with stones, pricked him with swords, and last of all, they burned him to ashes at the stake. Thus came Faithful to his end.

Now I saw that there stood behind the multitude a chariot and a couple of horses, waiting for Faithful. As soon as his adversaries had made an end of him, he was taken up into the chariot and straightway was carried up through the clouds, with the sound of trumpet, by the nearest way leading to the Celestial Gate.

But as for Christian, he had some respite, and was remanded back to prison. There he remained for some time, but He who overrules all things, having even the power of their rage in His own Hand, so brought it about, that Christian for all that time escaped them and went his way, singing as he went —

> *Well, Faithful, thou hast faithfully professed*
> *Unto thy Lord, with whom thou shalt be blessed.*
> *Sing, Faithful, sing, and let thy name survive;*
> *For though they killed thee, thou art yet alive.*

Notes on Chapter 13

[1] *John 4:36, Galatians 6:9*

[2] *I Corinthians 9:24-27* Do you not know that in a race all the runners compete, but only one receives the prize? So run that you may obtain it. Every athlete exercises self-control in all things. They do it to receive a perishable wreath, but we an imperishable. Well, I do not run aimlessly, I do not beat as one beating the air, but I pommel my body and subdue it, lest after preaching to others, I myself should be disqualified.

[3] *Revelation 3:11* I am coming soon: hold fast what you have, so that no one may seize your crown.

[4] Vanity means *empty,* hence this play on the word.

[5] *Ecclesiastes 1:14, 2:11,17; 11:8 and Isaiah 40:17* All nations are as nothing and emptiness before him, they are accounted by him as less than nothing and emptiness.

[6]*I Corinthians 5:9,10* I wrote you in my letter not to associate with immoral men; not at all meaning the immoral of this world, or the greedy and robbers, or idolaters, since you would need to go out of the world.

[7]*Matthew 4:8 and Luke 4:5-7*

[8]*I Corinthians 2:7,8* But we impart a secret and hidden wisdom of God, which God decreed before the ages for our glorification. None of the rulers of this age understood this; for if they had, they would not have crucified the Lord of glory.

[9]*Psalm 119:37* Turn my eyes from looking at vanities; and give me life in thy ways. *Philippians 3:19,20* Their end is destruction, their god is the belly, and they glory in their shame, with minds set on earthly things. But our commonwealth is in heaven, and from it we await a Savior, the Lord Jesus Christ.

[10]*Proverbs 23:23* Buy truth, and do not sell it; buy wisdom, instruction and understanding.

[11]*Hebrews 11:13-16* These all died in faith, not having received what was promised, but having seen it and greeted it from afar, and having acknowledged that they were strangers and exiles on earth. For people who speak thus make it clear that they are seeking a homeland. If they had been thinking of that land from which they had gone out, they would have had opportunity to return. But as it is, they desire a better country, that is, a heavenly one. Therefore God is not ashamed to be called their God, for he has prepared for them a city.

[12]Bunyan's original word *Pickthank* is obsolete. A sycophant is a toadying, servile informer who says exactly what is desired.

[13]*Exodus 1*

[14]*Daniel 3*

[15]*Daniel 6*

Encounter with By-ends and Friends

Christian did not leave the town alone, but was joined by one whose name was Hopeful, who had been made so by beholding Christian and Faithful in their words and behavior in their sufferings at the fair. This man joined himself to Christian, and, entering a brotherly covenant, told him that he would be his companion. Thus one died to bear testimony to the truth, and another rose out of his ashes to be a companion with Christian in his pilgrimage. This Hopeful also told Christian that there were many more of the men in the Fair who would take their time and follow after.

So I saw that soon after they had gotten out of the Fair, they overtook one going before them, whose name was By-ends. So they said to him, "What countryman, Sir? and how far do you go in this way?" He told them that he came from the town of Fairspeech and that he was going to the Celestial City. But he told them not his name.

"From Fairspeech!" said Christian. "Is there any good that lives there?"[1]

"Yes," said By-ends, "I hope so."

"Pray, Sir, what may I call you?" said Christian.

"I am a stranger to you and you to me," replied the other. "If you are going this way, I shall be glad of your company. If not, I must be content."

"This town of Fairspeech," said Christian, "I've heard of it. As I remember, they say it's a wealthy place."

"Yes, I will assure you that it is," said By-ends, "and I have very many rich relatives there."

"Pray who are your kindred there, if a man may be so bold?" asked Christian.

"Almost the whole town," said By-ends. "in particular, my Lord Turnabout, My Lord Timeserver, my Lord Fairspeech, from whose ancestors that town first took its name. Also, Mr. Smoothman, Mr. Facing-both-ways, Mr. Anything, and the parson of our parish, Mr. Twotongues, was my mother's own brother by father's side. To tell you the truth, I am become a gentleman of good quality, yet my great-grandfather was but a ferryman, looking one way and rowing another. I got most of my estate by the same occupation."

"Are you married?" asked Christian.

"Yes," answered By-ends, "and my wife is a very virtuous woman. She was my Lady Feigning's daughter, and therefore comes from a very honorable family. She comes from such a breeding that she knows how to carry it to all, even to prince and peasant. It is true we somewhat differ in religion from those of the stricter sort, yet in but two small points. First we never strive against the wind and tide; secondly, we are always most zealous when religion goes in his silver slippers. We love much to walk with him in the street if the sun shines and the people applaud him."

Christian stepped a little aside to his fellow, Hopeful, and said, "It comes to my mind that this is one By-ends of Fairspeech. If it is he, we have as true a knave in our company as dwells in these parts."

LADY FEIGNING'S DAUGHTER

Hopeful said, "Ask him. I think he should not be ashamed of his name."

So Christian came up with him again and said, "Sir, you talk as if you knew something more than all the world does. And if I do not miss the mark, I think I half guess your name. Are you not Mr. By-ends of Fairspeech?"

"This is not my name," answered the other. "It is indeed a nickname that has been given me by some who cannot abide me, and I must be content to bear it as a reproach, as other good men have borne theirs before me."

"But did you never give an occasion to men to call you by this name?" asked Christian.

"Never, never!" he replied. "The worst thing that I ever did to give them any occasion to call me this name was that I always had the luck to jump in my judgment with the present way of the times, whatever it was. It was my good luck to get good things in this way. But if things are thus cast upon me, let me count them a blessing, but let not the malicious load me because of it with reproaches."

"I thought indeed that you were the man I had heard of," Christian went on. "And to tell you what I think, I fear this name belongs to you more properly than you are willing to think it does."

By-ends answered, "Well! if you choose to think this, I cannot help it. You will find me a fair company-keeper if you will still have me as your associate."

Christian answered, "If you will go with us, you must go against wind and tide, and I gather this is against your opinion. You must also own your faith in its rags as well as when it is in silver slippers, and stand by it, too, when bound in irons, as well as when it walks the streets with applause."

By-ends answered quickly, "You must not impose, nor lord it over my faith. Leave me to my liberty, and let me go with you."

"Not one step further, unless you will do in this matter as we are prepared to do."

Then said By-ends, "I shall never desert my old principles, since they are harmless and profitable. If I may not go with you, I must do as I did before you overtook me — go by myself until some person overtakes me who will be glad of my company.''

Now I saw in my dream that Christian and Hopeful forsook him and kept their distance in front of him. But one of them looking back saw three men following Mr. By-ends, and behold, as they came up to him, he made them a very low bow,

BY-ENDS AND HIS FRIENDS

which they in turn returned to him. Their names were Mr. Hold-the-world, Mr. Money-love and Mr. Save-all, men that Mr. By-ends had been formerly acquainted with as school-boys together. In school they had all studied under Mr. Gripe-man, a schoolmaster in Lovegain, which is a market town in the county of Coveting, in the North. This schoolmaster taught them the art of getting, either by means of violence, flattery, lying or by putting on a disguise of religion. And these four men had attained much of the art of their master, so that they could each of them have kept such a school themselves.

Well, when they had, as I said, thus saluted each other, Mr. Money-love said to Mr. By-ends, "Who are they upon the road in front of us?" (for Christian and Hopeful were still in view).

"They are a couple of far countrymen," answered By-ends. "They after their mode are going on pilgrimage."

"Alas! Why did they not stay, that we might have had their good company?" asked Money-love. "For they, and we, and you, Sir, I hope, are all going on a pilgrimage."

"We are so, indeed," said By-ends. "But these men are so rigid and love so much their own notions, and so lightly esteem the opinions of others that, even though a man be ever so godly, if he does not jump with them in all things, they thrust him quite out of their company."

"That is bad," said Save-all, "but we read of some that are righteous overmuch. Such men's rigidness prevails with them to judge and condemn all but themselves. But, I pray, what and how many were the things in which you differed from them?"

By-ends said, "Why they, after their headstrong manner conclude that it is duty to rush on their journey in all kinds of weather, and I am for waiting for wind and tide. They are for hazarding all for God at a clap; and I am for taking all advantages to secure my life and estate. They are for holding their notions, though all other men are against them, but I am for religion in what, and so far as the times, and my safety, will bear it. They are for Religion when in rags and contempt, but I am for him when he walks in his golden slippers in the sunshine and with applause."

Mr. Hold-the-world spoke: "Aye and hold you there still, good Mr. By-ends. Because, for my part, I can count him but a fool who, having the liberty to keep what he has, shall be so unwise as to lose it. Let us be wise as serpents; it is best to make hay when the sun shines; you see how the bee lies still all winter, and stirs herself only when she can have profit with pleasure. God sends sometimes rain, and sometimes sun. If they be such fools to go through the first, let us yet be content to take fair weather along with us. For my part, I like that religion best that will stand with the security of God's good blessings to us. For who can imagine, if he is ruled by reason, since God has bestowed upon us the good things of this life, but that He would have us keep them for His sake? Abraham and Solomon grew rich in religion. And Job says that a good man shall lay up gold as dust. But he must not be such as the men before us, if they are as you describe them."

"I think that we are all agreed in this matter," said Mr. Save-all, "and therefore there need be no more words about it."

"No, there need be no more words about this matter indeed," added Mr. Money-love, "for he who believes neither Scripture nor reason (and you can see we have both on our side) neither knows his own liberty nor seeks his own safety."

Mr. By-ends spoke again: "My brethren, as you see we are all going on pilgrimage. For our better diversion from things that are bad, give me permission to propound you this question:

"Suppose a man, a minister, or a tradesman, etc., should have an advantage lying before him to get the good blessings of this life, and find that he can not come to them except (in appearance at least) by becoming extraordinarily zealous in some points of religion in which he has not shown any interest before. May he not use this new interest to attain his goal, and yet be an upright and honest man?"

"I see what you're asking," said Mr. Money-love, "and with these gentlemen's good leave, I will try to answer you. First, about the minister himself. Suppose a minister, a worthy man, possesses but a small congregation or parish, yielding him but a meager income.[2] Then it happens that he hears of a greater one by far, and has an opportunity to get it by being more studious, by preaching more frequently and zealously, and, because the temper of the people requires him to alter some of his principles, — for my part, I see no reason why a man should not do this, providing, of course, he has a call. In fact, I think he could do much more to advance himself and yet be an honest man. Why?

"First, because his desire for a greater benefice is certainly lawful since it is set before him by Providence. So then, he may get it if he can, making no question for conscience' sake.

"Secondly, since his desire for that benefice makes him more studious, a more zealous preacher, it makes him a better man. Yes, it makes him improve his talents, and this is certainly according to the mind of God.

"Third, as for his complying with the disposition of his people by departing from some of his principles in order to serve them, this proves that he is of a self-denying temperament and of a sweet and winning deportment, thus more fitted for his ministerial function.

"Finally, I conclude that a minister who changes a small for a great should not be judged as covetous. Rather, since he has improved his talents and shown industry by it, he should be counted as one who pursues his call and the opportunity put into his hand to do good.

"Now, to the second part of your question, which concerns the tradesman you mentioned. Suppose such a one has but a poor employment in the world, but by becoming religious may mend his lot, or perhaps get a rich wife, or more and far better customers to his shop. For my part, I see no reason why this should not lawfully be done, because, in the first place, to become religious is a virtue, no matter what a man's motive may be.

"Nor is it unlawful to get a rich wife, or more customers for a man's shop. Besides, the man who gets these by becoming religious gets that which is good from those who are good by becoming good himself. So here is a good wife, good customers, and good gain — and all these by becoming religious, which is also good. Therefore, to become religious to get all these, is a good and profitable design."

This answer which Mr. Money-love made to Mr. By-ends' question was highly applauded by them all, and they concluded all around that it was most wholesome and advantageous. Thinking that no man would be able to contradict this line of reasoning, and because Christian and Hopeful were still within call, they jointly agreed to pose the question to them as soon as they could reach them, since they had opposed Mr. By-ends before. So they called after them to wait until they could catch up with them. They concluded among themselves, however, as they went, that Mr. Hold-the-world should propound the question to them, because they wanted to avoid raising the heat of the argument again which had taken place with Mr. By-ends.

So they caught up with them, and after a short greeting,

Mr. Hold-the-world propounded the question to Christian and his companion, and bid them answer it if they could.

Then said Christian, "Even a babe in religion may answer ten thousand such questions. For if it is unlawful to follow

CHRISTIAN ANSWERS BY-ENDS AND HIS FRIENDS.

Christ for loaves (as it is in the sixth chapter of John), how much more abominable is it to make of him and religion a stalking-horse, to get and enjoy the world! Nor do we find any other than heathen, hypocrites, devils and witches who hold such opinions.

"Heathen, for when Hamor and Shechem wanted the

daughter and the cattle of Jacob, they saw that there was no way for them to get them except by becoming circumcised. They said to their companions, 'If every male of us be circumcised as are these Hebrews, shall not their cattle, their substance and every beast of theirs be ours?' Their daughter and their cattle were that which they sought to obtain, and their religion was a stalking-horse they made use of to come at them.[3]

"The hypocritical Pharisees were of the same persuasion. They made long prayers their pretense, but to get widow's houses was their intent, and from God greater damnation was their judgment for their misuse of religion.[4]

"Judas the devil was also of this opinion. He was religious for the money-bag, that he might take what was in it, but he was lost, cast away, — the very son of perdition.

"Simon Magus was of the same mind, for he would have had the Holy Spirit so that he might get money with the Spirit's power. His sentence from Peter's mouth was fitting.[5]

"I cannot get it out of my mind that a man who takes up religion for the world will throw away religion for the world; for so surely as Judas resigned the world in becoming religious, so surely did he also sell religion and his Master for the same. To answer the question affirmatively, as you have done, and to accept as authentic such an answer, is both heathenish, hypocritical and devilish; and you will be rewarded according to your works."

Then they stood staring at one another, but none had anything with which to answer Christian. Hopeful also approved of the soundness of Christian's answer, so there was a great silence among them. Mr. By-ends and his company then staggered and dropped back, so that Christian and Hopeful might outgo them.

Then said Christian to his fellow, "If these men cannot stand before the sentence of men, what will they do with the sentence of God? And if they are mute when dealt with by vessels of clay, what will they do when they are rebuked by the flames of a devouring fire?''

Then Christian and Hopeful went on ahead, leaving By-ends and his friends behind, until they came to a delicate plain called Ease. There they traveled with much content, but the plain was narrow, so they were soon through it. At the further side of that plain was a little hill called Lucre, and in that hill was a silver mine, which some of them who had formerly traveled that way, because of the rarity of it, had turned aside to see. But going too near the brink of the pit, the ground being treacherous under foot, they were thrown down and killed. Others had been maimed there and were unable to their dying day to be their own men again.

Then I saw in my dream that a little off the road, over against the silver mine, stood Demas, looking like a gentleman and calling out to the passers-by to come and see. He said to Christian and his fellow, "Ho! turn aside here, and I will show you a thing or two!''

"What thing is so deserving as to turn us out of the Way to see it?'' asked Christian.

"Here is a silver mine," replied the other, "and some people are digging in it for treasure. If you will come, with a little effort you may richly provide for yourselves."

Then said Hopeful, "Let us go see."

"Not I," said Christian. "I have heard of this place before now, and how many have been slain here. Besides that, this treasure is a snare to those who seek it, because it hinders them in their pilgrimage."

Then Christian called to Demas, saying, "Is not the place dangerous? Has it not hindered many in their pilgrimage?"[6]

"Not very dangerous," answered the other, "except to those who are careless." But Demas blushed as he spoke.

Then said Christian to Hopeful, "Let us not stir a step, but continue on our way."

"I will warrant you," said Hopeful, "that when By-ends comes up, if he has the same invitation as we, he will turn in there to see."

"No doubt of it," said Christian. "His principles lead him that way, and a hundred to one but he dies there."

Then Demas called again, saying, "But will you not come over and see?"

Then Christian roundly answered, "Demas, you are an enemy to the right ways of the Lord of this Way, and you have already been condemned for turning aside by one of his Majesty's judges.[7] Why, then, do you seek to bring us into the same condemnation? If we turn aside at all, our Lord the King will certainly hear of it and will put us to shame there where we would like to stand with boldness before Him."

Demas cried again that he also was one of their fraternity, and if they would tarry a little, he also would walk with them himself.

Christian said, "What is your name? Is it not the same by which I have called you?"

"Yes, my name is Demas, and I am a son of Abraham."

"I know you," said Christian. "Gehazi was your great-grandfather and Judas your father; and you have followed in their footsteps.[8] It is but a devilish plot you are trying to use. Your father was hanged as a traitor, and you deserve no better an end. Assure yourself, that when we come to the King, we will give Him word of this your behavior." Thus they went their way.

By this time By-ends and his companions were again in sight, and they, at the first call, went over to Demas. Now, whether they fell into the pit by looking over its brink, or whether they went down to dig, or whether they suffocated in the bottom by the noxious gases that commonly arise, I am not certain. But this I observed: that they were never seen again in the Way.

Now I saw that just on the other side of this plain, the Pilgrims came to a place where an old monument stood close by the highway. Seeing it, they were both concerned because of the strangeness of its form, for it seemed to them as though it was a woman transformed into the shape of a pillar. They stood looking and looking upon it, but could not for a time tell what they should make of it. At last Hopeful's eye caught something written above the head of the pillar, a writing in an unusual hand. Being no scholar, he called to Christian, (for he was learned) to see if he could pick out the meaning. Christian came, and after studying the letters a little while, found that it read thus: "Remember Lot's Wife." So he read it to his fellow. They concluded that this was the pillar of salt into which Lot's wife had been turned because she looked back with a covetous heart when she was fleeing from Sodom for safety.[9] This sudden and astounding sight gave rise to this conversation.

"What a timely sight this is," said Christian. "It came opportunely to us after the invitation which Demas gave us to come over to view the Hill Lucre. If we had gone over, as he wanted us to do, and as you were inclining to do, my brother, we would, for all I know, have been made like this woman — a spectacle for those who come after us to behold."

Hopeful said simply, "I am sorry that I was so foolish, and am made to wonder that I am not now in the same condition as Lot's wife. Where was there any difference between her sin and mine? She only looked back, and I had a desire to go and see. Let grace be adored, and let me be ashamed that ever such a thing should be in my heart!"

Christian continued: "Let us take notice of what we see

LOT'S WIFE

here, so that it might help us in the future. This woman escaped one judgment, for she fell not by the destruction of Sodom. But she was destroyed by another judgment, as we see she is turned into a pillar of salt.''

''True,'' said Hopeful; ''and she may be to us both caution and example. Caution, that we should shun her sin, or a sign of what judgment will overtake any who are not prevented by this caution. Korah, Dathan and Abiram with the two hundred and fifty men who perished in their sin became a sign and example to others to beware the same sin. But above all, I am impressed with one thing, namely, how Demas and his fellows can stand so confidently yonder to look for that treasure which this woman, but for looking back, was turned into a pillar of salt. For we do not read that she stepped even one foot out of the Way, yet the judgment which befell her made her an example within sight of where they are, for they cannot help seeing her if they only looked this way.''

''It is a thing to be wondered at,'' replied his friend. ''It shows that they have lost all hope. I cannot tell who to compare them to fittingly — perhaps they are like a man who picks pockets in the very presence of the judge, or who will cut purses right under the shadow of the gallows itself. It is said of the

CHRISTIAN AND HOPEFUL

men of Sodom that they were sinners exceedingly, because they were sinners before the Lord, that is, in his eyesight, regardless of the kindness that he had shown them. For the land of Sodom was like the garden of Eden had been. This, then, provoked Him the more to jealousy and made their plague as hot as the fire of the Lord out of heaven could make it. It is rationally to be concluded that such as these are who sin in sight of and despite of such examples as are set before them to warn them to the contrary, must be partakers of severest judgments.''

"Doubtless you have spoken the truth," Hopeful responded. "But what a mercy it is that neither you, but especially I, am not made myself the same example! This gives occasion to us to thank God, to fear before Him and always to remember Lot's wife.''

Notes on Chapter 14

[1]*Proverbs 26:25* When he speaks graciously, believe him not, for there are seven abominations in his heart.

[2]Bunyan's word is *benefice,* an ecclesiastical appointment that had a certain income attached, usually from an endowment. In the 17th and 18th centuries a parson was "settled" in a certain place, and it was looked on as a mark of unChristian ambition for a man to seek a better place. This attitude was also very powerful in America until the middle of the 19th century.

[3]*Genesis 34:20-23*

[4]*Luke 20:46,47*

[5]*Acts 8:19-22*

[6]*Joshua 7:20-21* Of a truth I have sinned against the Lord God of Israel, and this is what I did: when I saw among the spoil a beautiful mantle from Shinar, and two hundred shekels of silver, and a bar of gold weighing fifty shekels, then I covered them, and took them, and behold they are hidden in the earth inside my tent, with the silver underneath.

[7]*II Timothy 4:10* For Demas, in love with this present world, has deserted me . . . .

[8]*II Kings 5:20-27* Gehazi the servant of Elisha the man of God said, "See, my master has spared this Naaman the Syrian in not accepting from his hand what he brought. As the Lord lives, I will run after him and get something from him." So Gehazi followed Naaman, and when Naaman saw someone running after him, he alighted from the chariot to meet him, and said, "Is all well?" And he said, "All is well. My master sent me to say, 'There have just come to me from the hill country of Ephraim two young men of the sons of the prophets; pray, give them a talent of silver and two festal garments.' " And Naaman said, "Be pleased to accept two talents." And he urged him, and tied up two talents of silver in two bags, with two festal garments, and laid them upon two of his servants; and they carried them before Gehazi. And when he came to the hill, he took them from their hand, and put them in the house; and he sent the men away, and they departed. He went in and stood before his master, and Elisha said to him, "Where have you been, Gehazi?" And he said, "Your servant went nowhere." But he said to him, "Did I not go with you in spirit when the man turned from his chariot to meet you? Was it a time to accept money and garments, olive orchards and vineyards, sheep and oxen, menservants and maidservants? Therefore the leprosy of Naaman shall cleave to you and your descendants forever." So he went out of his presence a leper, as white as snow.

Matthew 26:14,15 Then one of the twelve, who was called Judas Iscariot, went to the chief priests and said, "What will you give me if I deliver him to you?" And they paid him thirty pieces of silver.

Matthew 27:3-5 When Judas, his betrayer, saw that he was condemned, he repented and brought back the thirty pieces of silver to the chief priests and elders, saying, "I have sinned in betraying innocent blood." They said, "What is that to us? See to it yourself." And throwing down the pieces of silver in the temple, he departed and he went and hanged himself.

[9]*Genesis 19:26* But Lot's wife behind him looked back, and she became a pillar of salt.

15

By-Path Meadow and Doubting Castle

I saw then, that they went on their way to a pleasant river, which King David called "the river of God," but John, "the river of the water of life."[1] Now their way lay just upon the bank of the river. Here Christian and his companion walked with great delight. They drank also of the water of the river, which was pleasant and enlivening to their weary spirits. Then, too, on the banks of this river, on either side, were green trees that bore all manner of fruit, and the leaves of the tree were good for medicine.[2] With the fruit of the trees they were very delighted, and the leaves they ate to prevent surfeits and other diseases that are common to those who get overheated in traveling. On either side of the river there was a meadow, curiously beautified with lilies and green all the year long. In this meadow they lay down and slept, for here they might lie down safely. When they awoke, they gathered again from the fruit of the trees, and drank again of the water of the river, and then lay down again to sleep.[3] They did this for several days and nights. And as they enjoyed the river, the meadow and the fruits they sang:

Behold how these bright crystal streams do glide
To comfort pilgrims by the highway side.
What pleasant fruit and leaves these trees do yield,
We would sell all, that we may buy this field.

THE PILGRIMS REST BY THE RIVER OF THE WATER OF LIFE.

So when they felt it was time to go on, they ate and drank again, and went on their way, for they were not as yet at their journey's end.

Now I beheld in my dream that they had not journeyed far until the river and the road for a time parted. They were very sorry about this, but did not dare go out of the way. Now the way from the river was rough, and their feet sore, because of their travels, "so the souls of the Pilgrims were much discouraged because of the Way."[4] Still, as they went on, they wished for a better way.

Now a little in front of them there was on the left hand of the road a meadow, and a stile to go over into it. That meadow is called By-path Meadow. Then Christian said to his fellow, "If this meadow lies alongside our way, let us go over into it." He went to the stile to seek, and behold, a path lay along by the way on the other side of the fence.

"It is just as I had hoped," said Christian. "Here is the easiest going; come, good Hopeful, and let us go over."

"But what if this path should lead us out of the Way?" asked Hopeful uncertainly.

CHRISTIAN AND HOPEFUL AT THE STILE
LEADING INTO BY-PATH MEADOW

"That is not likely," said the other. "Look, doesn't it go along by the way-side?"

So Hopeful, being persuaded by his fellow, went after him over the stile. When they were gone over and had gotten into the path, they found it very easy for their feet. On up ahead of them they spied another traveler whose name was Vain-confidence. They called after him and asked him whither that way led.

"To the Celestial Gate," he said.

"Look," said Christian, "did I not tell you so? By this you may see we are right."

So they followed and Vain-confidence went before them. But the night came on, and it grew very dark, so that they lost sight of him.

Vain-confidence, not seeing the way before himself, fell into a deep pit[5] which was made there on purpose by the prince of those grounds to catch vain-glorious fools with it, and was dashed to pieces with his fall.

Now Christian and Hopeful heard him fall. So they called to know what was happening, but there was no answer. All they heard was groaning.

Then Hopeful said, "Where are we now?"

His fellow-traveler said nothing, fearing that he had led his brother out of the Way. Now it began to rain and thunder and lighten in a very dreadful manner, and the water rose at great speed.

Hopeful groaned in himself, saying, "Oh, that I had kept on my way!"

"But who could have thought that this path should have led us out of the Way?" asked Christian defensively.

"I was afraid of it at the very beginning," said Hopeful. "I gave you that gentle caution. I wish now I had spoken plainer, and would have if you had not been older than I."

"Good brother, do not be offended," replied Christian. "I am sorry I have brought you out of the Way and that I have put you into such imminent danger. Forgive me, my brother. I did not do it of any evil intent."

"Be comforted, my brother, for I forgive you," said Hopeful. "Believe, too, that this shall be for our good."

Christian spoke again. "I am glad I have with me a merciful brother. But we must not stand here. Let us try to get back to the Way again."

"Let me go in front, brother," said Hopeful.

"No," said Christian, "you must let me go first, so that if there is any danger, I may be in it first, because it was by my counsel that we both went out of the Way."

"No," said Hopeful, "you shall not go first, for your mind is troubled and it may lead you out of the Way again."

Then, for their encouragement, they heard the voice of one saying, "Consider well the highway, the road by which you went.[6] Return."

But by this time the waters were greatly risen and the way of going back was very dangerous indeed. Then I thought that it is easier going out of the Way when we are in it than going back when we are out. Yet they ventured to go back, but it was so dark and the flood was so high that in their returning they almost drowned nine or ten times.

They could not, with all the skill they had, get back to the stile that night. So at last, lighting under a little shelter, they sat down there to wait for dawn to break. But being weary, they fell asleep.

Now there was, not far from the place where they lay a castle called Doubting Castle, whose owner was Giant Despair. It was in his grounds they were now sleeping. Getting up early in the morning and walking up and down in his fields, Giant Despair caught Christian and Hopeful asleep. With a grim

THE PILGRIMS FOUND ASLEEP BY GIANT DESPAIR

and surly voice, he waked them up and asked them where they came from and what they were doing in his grounds. They told him they were pilgrims and that they had lost their way. Then said the Giant, "You have this night trespassed on my grounds, and therefore you must go along with me."

So they were forced to go because he was stronger than they. They had but little to say, for they knew themselves to be at fault. The Giant, therefore, drove them before him, and put them into his castle in a very dark dungeon, nasty and stinking to the spirits of these two men.[7] Here they lay from Wednesday morning till Saturday night without one bit of bread or drop of drink, or light, or anyone to ask how they were doing. They were in a very bad state, far from friends and acquaintance. And in this condition Christian had the double sorrow of knowing that it was through his unwise counsel that they had been brought into this distress.

Now Giant Despair had a wife, and her name was Diffidence.[8] So when he had gone to bed, he told his wife what he had done, — that he had taken a couple of prisoners and cast them into his dungeon for trespassing his grounds. He asked her what he should do further to them. So she asked him what they were, whence they came and whither they were bound, and he told her. Then she counseled him that when he arose in the morning he should beat them without any mercy. So,

GIANT DESPAIR BEATS THE PILGRIMS, AND LEAVES THEM
TO MOURN UNDER THEIR DISTRESS.

when he arose the next day, he got him a grievous crab-tree cudgel and went down into the dungeon to them, and there began first to berate them as if they were dogs, although they never gave him a word to annoy him. Then he fell upon them and beat them fearfully, in such a way that they were not able to help themselves, or even to turn themselves upon the floor. This done, he withdrew and left them to condole their misery and to mourn under their distress. So all that day they spent the time in nothing but sighs and bitter lamentations. The next night, Diffidence, talking with her husband about them further and finding that they were still alive, advised him to counsel them to do away with themselves. So when morning was come, he went to them in a surly manner as before, and perceiving that they were very sore with the stripes he had given them the day before, he told them that since they were never likely to get out of that place, their only hope was to make an end of themselves, either with knife, halter or poison. "For why," said he, "should you choose life, seeing it is attended with so much bitterness?"

But they begged him to let them go. With that he looked fiercely at them and rushing at them would doubtless have made an end of them himself, but instead fell into one of his fits, which he sometimes did in sunny weather, and lost for a time the use of his head. Wherefore, he withdrew and left them as before to consider what to do. Then the prisoners consulted between themselves, whether it was best to take his counsel or no. Thus they began to discourse: —

"Brother," said Christian, "what shall we do? The life that we now live is miserable. For my part I do not know whether it is best to live thus, or to die out of hand. 'My soul would choose strangling rather than life,'[9] and the grave is more easy for me than this dungeon. Shall we be ruled by this Giant?"

"Our present condition is dreadful indeed," answered his

companion. "Death would be far more welcome to me than to remain this way forever. Yet, let us consider, the Lord of the country to which we are going has said, 'Thou shalt do no murder,'[10] no, not to another man's person; much more, then, are we forbidden to take his counsel to kill ourselves. Besides, he who kills another can but commit murder upon his body. But for one to kill himself is to kill body and soul at once. Moreover, my brother, you talk of the ease of the grave; but have you forgotten the hell to which for certain murderers go? For 'no murderer has eternal life.'[11] And let us consider again that all the law is not in the hand of Giant Despair. Others, so far as I can understand, have been taken by him as well as we, and yet have escaped out of his hand. Who knows but that God who made the world may cause that Giant Despair to die? or that at some time or other he may forget to lock us in? or that he may, in a short time, have another of his fits in front of us and may lose the use of his old limbs? and if ever that should come to pass again, for my part, I am resolved to pluck up in heart and to try my utmost to get out from under his hand. I was a fool that I did not try to do it before, but, however, my brother, let us be patient and endure a while. The time may come that may give us a happy release. But let us not be our own murderers."

With these words, Hopeful was able to moderate the mind of his brother, so they continued together in the dark that day, in their sad and doleful condition.

Well, towards evening, the Giant went down into the dungeon again to see if his prisoners had taken his counsel. But when he came to them he found them alive; and truly, alive was all, for now, for lack of bread and water, and because of the wounds they had received under his beating, they could do little but breathe. But, I say, he found them alive. At this he fell into a dreadful rage and told them that since they had disobeyed his counsel, it would be worse for them than if they had never been born.

At this they trembled greatly, and I think that Christian fainted; but coming a little to himself again, they renewed their discourse about the Giant's counsel; and whether even yet they had best take it or not. Now Christian again seemed to be for doing it, but Hopeful again made reply, as follows:

"My brother," said he, "do you not remember how valiant and brave you have been heretofore? Apollyon could not crush you nor could all that you heard or saw or felt in the Valley of the Shadow of Death. What hardship, terror and amazement have you already gone through! And are you now nothing but fear? You see that I am in the dungeon with you, a far weaker man by nature than you are; also, this Giant has wounded me as well as you, and has cut off the bread and water from my mouth; and with you I mourn without the light. But let us exercise a little more patience! Remember how you played the man at Vanity Fair and were neither afraid of the chain, nor cage, nor yet of bloody death. Let us then, at least to avoid the shame that is so unbecoming for a Christian to be found in, bear up with patience as well as we can."

Now night had come again, and the Giant and his wife were in bed again when she asked him about the prisoners and if they had taken his counsel. He replied, "They are sturdy rogues. They choose rather to bear all hardship than to make away with themselves." Then said she, "Take them into the castle-yard tomorrow, and show them the bones and skulls of those that you have already dispatched, and make them believe that before a week comes to an end, you will also tear them in pieces as you have done their fellows before them."

So when the morning came, the Giant went to them again and took them into the castle-yard, and showed them, as his wife had bidden him. "These," said he, "were once pilgrims as you are, and they trespassed in my grounds as you have done. And when I thought fit, I tore them in pieces, and so, within ten days, I will do you! Go! Get you down to your den again!'' And with that he beat them all the way back to the dungeon. They lay, therefore, all day on Saturday in a lamentable state as before.

Now when night was come, and when Mrs. Diffidence and her husband the Giant, were gotten into bed, they began to renew their discussion concerning their prisoners. And the old Giant wondered why he could not either by blows or by counsel bring them to an end. With that his wife replied; "I fear," said she, "that they live in hope that someone will come to relieve them, or that they have picklocks about them by the means of which they hope to escape."

"And do you say so, my dear?" said the Giant. "Then I will search them in the morning."

Well, on Saturday, about midnight, they began to pray, and continued in prayer till almost break of day.

Now, a little before it was day, good Christian, as one half-amazed, brake out in this passionate speech: "What a fool," said he, "am I, thus to lie in a stinking dungeon when I may as well walk at liberty! I have a key in my bosom, called Promise, that will, I am persuaded, open any lock in Doubting Castle."

Then said Hopeful, "That is good news, good brother; pluck it out of your bosom and try!"

Then Christian pulled it out of his bosom, and began to try at the dungeon door. The bolt of the door, as he turned the key, gave way and the door flew open with ease, and both Christian and Hopeful came out of the dungeon. Then Christian went to the outward door that led into the castle-yard, and with his key opened that door also. After this he went to the iron gate, for that too had to be opened. That lock went damnably hard, yet the key did open it. They thrust open the gate to make their escape with speed, but that gate made such a creaking noise as it opened that it waked Giant Despair, who hastily rose to pursue his prisoners, felt his limbs to fail as his fits took him again, and thus could by no means go after them! Then they went on and came to the King's highway, and so were safe, because they were out of the jurisdiction of the Giant.

CHRISTIAN AND HOPEFUL ESCAPE FROM THE DUNGEON
OF GIANT DESPAIR.

Now when they got over the stile, they began to contrive with themselves what they could do at that stile to prevent others who came after them from falling into the hands of Giant Despair. They agreed to erect a marker there and to engrave upon the side of it this sentence: "Over this stile is the way to Doubting Castle, which is kept by Giant Despair, who despises the King of the Celestial Country, and seeks to destroy His holy pilgrims." Many, therefore, who came after, read what was written and escaped the danger. Having erected the marker, they went on their way, singing,

> *Out of the way we went and found*
> *We tread upon forbidden ground.*
> *Let them who follow have a care,*
> *Lest heedlessness make them unaware,*
> *And they in Doubting Castle fare*
> *As prisoners of the Giant Despair.*

Notes on Chapter 15

[1]*Psalm 65:9b* The river of God is full of water; thou providest their grain, for so thou hast prepared it. *Revelation 22:1* Then he showed me the river of the water of life, bright as crystal, flowing from the throne of God and of the Lamb.

[2]*Ezekiel 47:12* And on the banks, on both sides of the river, there will grow all kinds of trees for food. Their leaves will not wither, nor their fruit fail, but they will bear fresh fruit every month, because the water for them flows from the sanctuary. Their fruit will be for food, and their leaves for healing. *Revelation22:2b* Also, on either side of the river, the tree of life, with its twelve kinds of fruit, yielding its fruit each month; and the leaves of the tree were for the healing of the nations.

[3]*Psalm 23:2* He makes me to lie down in green pastures. He leads me beside still waters. (Hebrew — *the waters of rest.*) *Isaiah 14:30* And the first-born of the poor will feed, and the needy will lie down in safety.

[4] *Numbers 21:4*

[5]*Isaiah 9:16* For those who lead this people lead them astray, and those who are led by them are swallowed up.

[6]*Jeremiah 31:21*

[7] *Psalm 88:18* Thou hast caused lover and friend to shun me; my companions are in darkness.

[8] Diffidence meant *distrustful.* Note how this fits into what went on.

[9] *Job 7:15*

[10] *Exodus 20:13; Deuteronomy 5:17; Matthew 5:21; Romans 13:9*

[11] *I John 3:15*

The Pilgrims Reach the
Delectable Mountains

Christian and Hopeful continued on their way till they came to the Delectable Mountains, which belong to the Lord of that hill of which we have spoken before. So they went up to the mountains to behold the gardens and orchards, the vineyards and fountains of water. There they drank and washed themselves and freely ate of the vineyards.

Now there were on the tops of these mountains Shepherds feeding their flocks, and they stood by the side of the highway. The Pilgrims went to them, and leaning on their staves (as is common with weary pilgrims when they stand to talk with anyone by the road), they asked, "Whose Delectable Mountains are these? And whose are the sheep that feed on them?"

"These mountains are Immanuel's Land," replied the Shepherds. "And they are within sight of His city. The sheep are His, too, and He laid down His life for them."[1]

"Is this the way to the Celestial City?" queried Christian.

"Indeed," replied the Shepherds, "you are right on your way."

"And how far is it from here?" asked Christian.

THE PILGRIMS WELCOMED BY THE SHEPHERDS
ON THE DELECTABLE MOUNTAINS

"Too far for any but those who shall arrive there indeed," was the answer.

"Is the Way safe or dangerous?"

"Safe for those for whom it is safe," was the answer; "but the transgressors shall fall in it."[2]

Christian continued his inquiry: "Is there, in this place, any relief for Pilgrims that are weary in the Way?"

The Shepherd replied, "The Lord of these mountains has given us charge not to be 'forgetful to entertain strangers,'[3] so, the good of the country is before you."

The Shepherds perceived that they were wayfaring men and began to ask them the same questions that others had asked along their pilgrimage, such as, "Where did you come from? How did you get into the Way? And by what means have you so persevered in the Way?

"For but few of them that begin on pilgrimage ever reach these mountains," they said sadly. But when the Shepherds had heard their answers, they were pleased with them, and looked very lovingly on them, saying, "Welcome to the Delectable Mountains."

The names of the Shepherds are Knowledge, Experience, Watchful and Sincere. They took the Pilgrims by the hand and led them to their tents, making them partake of that which was ready for them to eat. They said to them, "We would that you should stay here awhile, to be acquainted with us, and even more, to solace yourselves with the good of these Delectable Mountains."

Christian and Hopeful said that they were content to stay, so they went to their rest that night, because it was very late.

The next morning the Shepherds called Christian and Hopeful to walk with them on the mountains. So they went forth with them and walked awhile, having a pleasant prospect on every side. Then said the Shepherds one to another, "Shall we show these Pilgrims some wonders?" So when they had concluded to do it, they took them first to the top of a hill called Error, which was very steep on its furthest side, and bid them look down at the bottom. As Christian and Hopeful looked down, they saw at the bottom several men dashed all to pieces by a fall they had from the top.

"What does this mean?" asked Christian.

The Shepherds answered, "Have you not heard of them who were made to err by listening to Hymeneus and Philetus, as concerning the resurrection of the body?"[4]

They answered, "Yes."

Then the Shepherds continued, "Those you see dashed in

pieces at the bottom of this mountain are they; and they have continued to this day unburied, as you see, for an example to others to take heed how they climb too high, or how they come too near the brink of this mountain.''

They went on to the top of another mountain, the name of which is Caution, and bid them look afar off. When they did this, they thought they saw several men walking up and down among the tombs they could see in the distance. They could tell, as they watched, that the men were blind, because they stumbled upon the tombs and gravestones as they walked, and could not find their way out from them.

''What does this mean?'' Christian asked.

''Did you not see a little below these mountains a stile that

THE VICTIMS OF GIANT DESPAIR AMONG THE TOMBS

led into a meadow on the left side of this Way?" asked the Shepherds.

They answered, "Yes."

Then said the Shepherds, "From that stile there goes a path that leads directly to Doubting Castle, which is kept by Giant Despair, and these people (pointing to them among the tombs), came once on pilgrimage as you do now, till they came to that same stile. And because the right Way was rough in that place, they chose to go out of it into that meadow, and there were taken by Giant Despair, cast into Doubting Castle, and after they had been kept in the dungeon, he put their eyes out and led them among these tombs, where he has left them to wander to this very day. This is to fulfill the saying, "He who wanders out of the way of understanding shall remain in the assembly of the dead."[5]

Then Christian and Hopeful looked at one another, with tears running down their cheeks, but said nothing to the Shepherds.

Then I saw in my dream, that the Shepherds took them to another place, where there was a door in the side of a hill. They opened the door and bid them look in. They saw within that it was very dark and smoky, and they thought that they heard a rumbling noise, as of fire, and a cry of some tormented and that they smelt the scent of brimstone.

Then said Christian, "What does this mean?"

The Shepherds told them, "This is a by-way to hell, a way that hypocrites go in at; for instance, those who sell their birthright, as Esau did; such as sell their Master, as Judas did; such as blaspheme the Gospel, as Alexander;[6] and who lie and deceive, with Ananias and Sapphira."[7]

Then Hopeful observed to the Shepherds: "I see that all these had on them a show of pilgrimage, as we have now, did they not?"

"Yes, and held it a long time, too," answered the Shepherds.

"How far might they go on in pilgrimage in their day, since they were, in spite of their travels, miserably cast away?"

"Some further, and some not so far as these mountains," was the reply.

Then the Pilgrims said one to another, "We have need to cry to the Strong for strength."

"Aye," said the Shepherds, "and you will have need to use it when you have it, too!"

By this time the Pilgrims had a desire to go on, and the Shepherds agreed that they should, so they walked together towards the end of the mountains. Then the Shepherds said one to another, "Let us here show to the Pilgrims the gates of the Celestial City, if they have the skill to look through our perspective glass. The Pilgrims were happy to accept the suggestion, so they led them to the top of a high hill, called Clear, and gave them their glass to look.

Then they tried to look, but the remembrance of the last thing that the Shepherds had shown them made their hands tremble, so that they could not look steadily through the glass. Yet they thought they saw something like the gate and also some of the glory of the place.

When they were about to depart, one of the Shepherds gave them a sketch of the Way. Another of them bid them to beware of the Flatterer. A third warned them to take heed that they sleep not on the Enchanted Ground. And a fourth bid them Godspeed.

And so the Pilgrims went on their way.

Notes on Chapter 16

[1] *John 10:11*
[2] *Hosea 14:9*

[3]*Hebrews 13:2*

[4]*II Timothy 2:17,18* Their talk will eat like gangrene. Among them are Hymenaeus and Philetus, who have swerved from the truth by holding that the resurrection is past already. They are upsetting the faith of some.

[5]*Proverbs 21:16*

[6]*II Timothy 4:14* Alexander the coppersmith did me great harm: the Lord will requite him for his deeds.

[7]*Acts 5:1-5*

17

Ignorance and Little-faith

he Pilgrims went down the mountains along the highway towards the Celestial City. Now, a little below these mountains, on the left side, lies the country of Conceit. From that country there was a little crooked lane coming into the road on which the Pilgrims walked. Here they met with a very brisk lad who came out of that country, whose name was Ignorance. So Christian asked him from what parts he came, and whither he was going.

"Sir, I was born in the country that lies off there a little on the left side," answered the young man, "and I am going to the Celestial City."

"But how do you think to get in at the gate?" asked Christian. "You may find some difficulty there."

"I should get in as other good people do," said he.

Christian continued, "But what have you to show at that gate, that may cause that the gate should be opened to you?"

Ignorance replied, "I know my Lord's will, and I have lived a good life. I pay every man his own, I pray, fast, pay tithes, and give alms, and have left my country for the one to which I am going."

Christian persisted: "But you did not come in at the wicket-gate at the head of the Way! You came in through that same crooked lane there, and I fear, no matter what you may think of yourself, when the day of reckoning comes, you will have it laid to your charge that you are a thief and a robber, instead of getting admittance to the City."[1]

"Gentlemen, you are utter strangers to me, and I don't know you," replied Ignorance condescendingly. "Please be content to follow the religion of your country, and I will follow the religion of mine. I hope all will be well. And as for that gate you talk of, all the world knows that it is a great distance from our country. I cannot think that any man in all our area so much as knows the way to it, nor need they care whether they do or not, since we have, as you see, a fine, pleasant green lane that comes down from our country, the nearest route into this Way."

When Christian saw that the man was "wise in his own conceit," he whispered to Hopeful, "There is more hope of a fool than of him."[2] And he added, "When he who is a fool walks by the way, his wisdom fails him, and he says to everyone that he is a fool.[3] Shall we talk further with him, or leave him behind at the present to think over what he has already heard, and then stop again to speak to him afterward, to see if in any way we might do him any good?"

Hopeful said, "I do not think it is good to say everything to him at once. Let us pass him by, if you will, and talk to him later on, even as he is able to bear it."

So they both went on, and Ignorance followed behind. When they had gone a little way, they entered into a very dark lane, where they met a man whom seven devils had bound with seven strong cords; and they were carrying him back to the door that they had seen on the side of the hill.[4] Now good Christian began to tremble again, as did his companion Hope-

IGNORANCE

ful. Yet as the devils led away the man, Christian looked to see if he knew him. He thought it might be one Turn-away, who lived in the town of Apostasy. But he did not clearly see his face, for the man's head hung down like that of a thief who has been caught. After he had passed, however, Hopeful looked back and saw on the man's back a paper with this writing: "Wanton professor and damnable apostate."[5]

As they went on, Christian remarked to his companion, "I remember what was told me of a thing that happened to a good man in this area. His name was Little-faith, but he was a good man and lived in the town of Sincere. The thing was this: at the entrance of this passage there came down from Broadway Gate a lane called Dead Man's Lane, so called because of the murders that occurred there so often. This Little-faith was going on pilgrimage, as we do now, and chanced to sit down there and fell asleep. Now it happened at that time that there came down the lane from Broadway Gate, three sturdy rogues — Faint-heart, Mistrust and Guilt. They were brothers, and spying Little-faith as he sat there, they came galloping up with all speed. He was just waking up, getting ready to resume his journey. So they all rushed to him and with threatening language told him to stand up. At this Little-faith looked white as a ghost, and had neither the strength to fight or to fly. Then said Faint-heart, 'Hand over your purse.'

"Little-faith cried out, 'Thieves! Thieves!' And with that, Guilt, with a great club that was in his hand, struck Little-faith on the head, and with that blow, felled him flat to the ground, where he lay bleeding as though he would bleed to death. All this while the thieves stood by. But at last, hearing someone on the road, and fearing lest it should be one Great-grace who dwells in the city of Good-confidence, they betook themselves to their heels, and left this good man to shift for himself. Now after a while, Little-faith came to himself, and got up and began to scramble on his way again. That was the story I heard."

"Did they take from him everything he had?" asked Hopeful.

"No," said Christian. "The place where his jewels were

LITTLE-FAITH ROBBED

they never ransacked, so he kept those still. But as I was told, the good man was very much grieved at his loss, because the thieves got most of his spending-money. That which they did not get, as I said, were jewels. He also had a little odd money left, but hardly enough to bring him to his journey's end.[6] No, if I was not misinformed, he was forced to beg as he went, to keep himself alive. He was not free to sell his jewels. But he had to beg and do what he could, and he went, as we say, with many a hungry belly the most part of the rest of the way."

"But is it not a wonder that they did not get from him his certificate by which he was to be admitted to the Celestial City?" asked Hopeful.

"It is a wonder," said the other. "But they did not get that, though they did not miss it through any cleverness of his; for he, so dismayed by their coming upon him, had neither the power nor skill to hide anything. So it was more by good Providence than by any endeavor of his that they missed any good thing."

"But it must be a comfort to him that they did not get his jewels from him," observed Hopeful.

"It might have been great comfort to him if he had used it as he ought," said Christian. "But they who told me the story said that he made but little use of it all the rest of the way, and that because of his dismay in losing his money, he forgot the fact that they had not stolen his jewels for a great part of the rest of his journey. And they said that when at any time the occurrence came to his mind and he began to be comforted with what was not lost, fresh thoughts of his loss would come on him again, and those thoughts would swallow him up."[7]

"Alas! poor man!" exclaimed Hopeful. "This could not but be a great grief to him."

"Grief! yes, a grief indeed," Christian shook his head sadly. "Would it not have been so to any of us if we had been robbed and wounded as he was — and in that strange place, too? It is a wonder he did not die with grief, poor heart. I was told that he strewed almost all the rest of the way with nothing but doleful and bitter complaints, telling all who overtook him in the Way, where he was robbed and how, who they were who did it, and what he lost, how he was wounded, and that he hardly escaped with his life."

Hopeful spoke again. "Is it not a wonder that his need did not make him decide to sell or pawn some of his jewels, so that he might have what he needed to make his journey more tolerable?"

"You talk like one with a shell on his head to this very

LITTLE-FAITH'S GRIEF FOR HIS LOSS

day!'' retorted Christian. ''For what should he pawn them, or to whom should he sell them? In all that country where he was robbed, his jewels were not valued, nor did he desire that relief which could be gained from such a bargain. Besides, if his jewels had been missing when he arrived at the gate of the Celestial City, he would have been excluded from an inheritance there, and that would have been worse to him than the appearance and villainy of ten thousand thieves, and that he knew well enough!''

''Why are you so sharp, my brother?'' asked Hopeful. ''Esau sold his birthright, and that for a mere mess of pottage, and that birthright was his greatest jewel. If he, why might not Little-faith do so too?''[8]

Christian replied, ''Esau did sell his birthright indeed, and so do many besides him. By so doing they exclude themselves from the chief blessing, as that despicable man did. But you must see a difference between Esau and Little-faith, and also between their conditions. Esau's belly was his god, but Little-faith's belly was not so. Esau's need lay in his fleshly appetite; Little-faith's did not so. Besides, Esau could see no further than to the fulfilling of his lusts: 'Behold, I am about to die; of what use is a birthright to me?'[9] But Little-faith, though it was his lot to have but a little faith, was by his little faith kept from such extravagances, and was made to see and prize his jewels too much to sell them as Esau sold his birthright. You do not read anywhere that Esau had faith, no, not so much as a little. Therefore it is no marvel if, where the flesh only bears sway, as it will in any man where there is no faith to resist it, if he should sell his birthright, his soul and everything — and that to the devil of hell! For it is with such as it is with the wild donkey, as Jeremiah reminds us.[10] When their minds are set upon their lusts they will have them, whatever the cost. But Little-faith was of another temper. His mind was on things divine. His livelihood was on things that were spiritual and from above. Therefore to what end should he who is of such a temper sell his jewels, even if there had been anyone to buy them, to fill his mind with empty things? Will a man give a penny to fill his stomach with hay, or can you persuade the turtle-dove to live on garbage like the crow?

Though faithless ones can for their fleshly lusts, pawn or mortgage or sell what they have and themselves outright to boot, yet those who have faith, saving faith — though but a little of it — cannot do so. Here, my brother, is your mistake!''

When Christian ceased his discourse, Hopeful looked at him and spoke again. ''I acknowledge my mistake, but your severe words almost made me angry!''

Christian smiled. ''Why, I only compared you to some of the birds of the brisker sort, who will run to and fro with the shell on their heads. But pass that by, and consider the matter under discussion and all will be well between you and me.''

''But, Christian, these three fellows, I am sure in my heart, are but a company of cowards,'' said Hopeful. ''Would they otherwise have run, do you think, as they did when they heard the sound of someone approaching on the road? Why did not Little-faith pluck up a greater heart? He might, I think, have stood one encounter with them and then yield, if there was no other remedy.''

''Many have said they are cowards,'' answered his brother. ''But few have found it so in the time of trial. As for a great heart, Little-faith had none. I gather from what you say, my brother, that you are but for a fight and then to yield. Since that is 'the height of your stomach,' as they say, even now when they are at a distance from you, you might have second thoughts if suddenly they should appear to you as they did to him.

''But consider again, they are but traveling thieves, they serve under the king of the bottomless pit, who will, if he has to, come to their aid himself, and his voice is as the roaring of a lion.[11] I myself have been engaged as this Little-faith was, and I found it a terrible thing. These three villains set upon me, and when I began, like a Christian, to resist, they gave but a call and in came their master. I would, as the saying is, have given my life for a penny. But as God would have it, I was clothed with strong armor. But even though I was so equipped, I found it hard work to quit myself like a man. No man can tell what in that combat may be in store for us except one who has been in the battle himself.''

Hopeful was persistent. "But they ran, you see, when they but supposed that one Great-grace was on the way.''

"That's true,'' said Christian. "They have often fled, both they and their master, when Great-grace appeared. But that is no wonder, for he is the King's Champion. But I think you will recognize some difference between Little-faith and the King's Champion. All the King's subjects are not His champions, nor can they do such feats of war as He when they are tried. Is it fitting to think that a young boy should handle Goliath as David did? Or that there should be the strength of an ox in a wren? Some are strong, some are weak. Some have great faith, some have little. This man was one of the weak, and because of it, he went to the wall.''

"I wish it had been Great-grace for the sake of those rogues!'' exclaimed Hopeful.

Christian saw that he had not yet gotten his point across. "Even if it had been, he might have had his hands full," he said. "I must tell you that, though Great-grace is excellent in using his weapons, and that so long as he keeps them at sword's point can do well enough with them, yet, if Faint-heart, Mistrust or Guilt get within him, it goes hard with him, and they will knock him down. Anyone who looks carefully on Great-grace's face will see scars and cuts there that easily show what I say. I heard that he once said, and that when he was in combat, 'We despaired even of life.'[12] How did those strong scoundrels and their fellows make David groan, mourn and roar? Peter, you remember, said he would be faithful to the end. Yet though some call him the prince of the apostles, these scoundrels handled him so that they made him at last afraid of a sorry girl.

"Besides, their king is at their whistle. He is never out of hearing, and if at any time they are getting the worst of it, he will, if possible, come to help them. Of him it is said, 'Though the sword reaches him, it does not avail; nor the spear, the dart or the javelin. He counts iron as straw and bronze as rotten wood. The arrow cannot make him flee; for him slingstones are turned to stubble. Clubs are counted as stubble; he laughs at the rattle of javelins.'[13] What can a man do in this case? It is true, if a man could at every turn have Job's horse, and had skill and courage to ride him, he might do notable things; 'for his neck is clothed with thunder, he will not be afraid of the grasshopper; his majestic snorting is terrible. He paws in the valley and exults in his strength; he goes out to meet the weapons. He laughs at fear and is not dismayed; he does not turn back from the sword. Upon him rattle the quiver, the flashing spear and the javelin. With fierceness and rage he swallows the ground; he cannot stand still at the sound of the trumpet. When the trumpet sounds, he says, "Aha!" He smells the battle from afar, the thunder of the captains, and the shouting.'[14]

"But for such lowly servants as you and I are, let us never desire to meet with an enemy, nor brag as though we could do better when we hear that others have been foiled, nor be pleased at the thoughts of our own manly strength! For such commonly come off the worst when they are tried. Look at Peter, whom I mentioned before. He swaggered — yes, he would, he would, as his vain mind prompted him to say he would do better and stand more for his Master than all men. But who was so bested and run down by these villains as he?

"When we hear that such robberies are done on the King's highway, two things become us to do: first, to go out armored and to be sure to take a shield with us; for it was for want of that, that the one who attacked Leviathan, as I described earlier from the book of Job, could not make him yield. Indeed, if we do not have our shield, he fears us not at all. Therefore another has said, 'Above all, taking the shield of faith, wherewith you will be able to quench all the fiery darts of the wicked.'[15] It is good, too, (in the second place) that we ask the King for a convoy, yes, that He will go with us Himself. This made David rejoice when in the Valley of the Shadow of Death; and Moses was rather for dying where he stood than go one step without his God.[16] Oh, my brother, if He will but go along with us, what need is there to be afraid of ten thousands that shall set themselves against us?[17] But without Him, the proud helpers 'fall under the slain.'[18]

"For my part, I have been in the battle before now; and although I am still alive, as you see, through the goodness of Him who is best, I cannot boast of my manhood. I shall be glad if I meet with no more such brunts; though I fear we have not gotten beyond all danger. However, since the lion and the bear have not as yet devoured me, I hope God will also deliver us from the next enemy.' "[19]

Notes on Chapter 17

[1]*John 10:1* Truly, truly I say to you, he who does not enter the sheepfold by the door but climbs in by another way, that man is a thief and a robber.

[2]*Proverbs 26:12*

[3]*Ecclesiastes 10:3*

[4]*Matthew 12:45* Then he goes and brings with him seven more spirits more evil than himself, and they enter and dwell there; and the last state of that man becomes worse than the first. *Proverbs 5:22* The iniquities of the wicked ensnare him, and he is caught in the cords of his own sin.

[5]"Professor" here is one who professes religious faith.

[6]*I Peter 4:18* And if a righteous man is scarcely saved, where will the impious and sinner appear?

[7]*I Peter 1:5-9* Who by God's power are guarded through faith for a salvation ready to be revealed in the last time. Rejoice in this, though now for a little while you may have to suffer various trials, so that the genuineness of your faith more precious than gold which though perishable is tested by fire, may redound to praise and glory and honor at the revelation of Jesus Christ. Without having seen him you love him; though you do not now see him you believe in him and rejoice with unutterable and exalted joy. As the outcome of your faith you obtain the salvation of your souls.

[8]*Hebrews 12:16* See that no one be immoral or irreligious like Esau, who sold his birthright for a single meal.

[9]*Genesis 25:32*

[10]*Jeremiah 2:24*

[11]*Psalm 7:1,2* O Lord my God, in thee do I take refuge; save me from all my pursuers, and deliver me, lest like a lion they rend me, dragging me away, with none to rescue. *I Peter 5:8* Be sober, be watchful. Your adversary the devil prowls around like a roaring lion, seeking someone to devour.

[12]*II Corinthians 1:8* We were so utterly, unbearably crushed that we despaired of life itself.

[13]*Job 41:26-29*

[14]*Job 39:19-25*

[15]*Ephesians 6:16*

[16]*Exodus 33:15*

[17]*Psalm 3:5-8* I lie down and sleep; I wake up again, for the Lord sustains me. I am not afraid of ten thousands of people who have set themselves against me round about . . . For thou dost smite all my enemies on the cheek, thou dost break the teeth of the wicked. Deliverance belongs to the Lord; thy blessing be upon thy people! *Psalm 27:1-3* The Lord is my light and my salvation; whom shall I fear? The Lord is the stronghold of my life; of whom shall I be afraid? When evildoers assail me, uttering slanders against me, my adversaries and foes, they shall stumble and fall. Though an host encamp against me, my heart shall not fear; though war arise against me, yet I will be confident.

[18]*Isaiah 10:4*

[19]*I Samuel 17:37* And David said, ''The Lord who delivered me from the paw of the lion and from the paw of the bear, will deliver me from the hand of this Philistine.''

The Pilgrims Learn

a Lesson the Hard Way

So they went on and Ignorance followed. They went then till they came to a place where they saw a road dividing off from their Way. Both ways seemed to lie straight, and they did not know which way to take. So they stood still to consider. As they were thinking about the way, behold a man covered with a very light robe came to them and asked them why they stood there. They answered that they were going to the Celestial City, but did not know which of these ways to take.

"Follow me," said the man, "for it is thither that I am going."

So they followed him in the way that divided off from the Way in which they traveled. As they went, the road turned and turned by degrees, so that before they knew it, their faces were turned away from the City. Yet they followed him. But by and by, before they were aware, he led them both within the compass of a net in which they were both so entangled that they knew not what to do. With that, the white robe fell off the man's back, and they saw where they were. They lay there crying for some time, for they could not get themselves out.

Then said Christian to his fellow, "Now do I see myself in error. Did not the Shepherds bid us beware of the flatterers? As in the saying of the wise men, so we have found it this day, 'A man who flatters his neighbor spreads a net for his feet.' "[1]

"They also gave us a sketch of directions about the Way," remembered Hopeful. "But somehow we have forgotten to look at it, and have not kept ourselves from the paths of the destroyer. Here David was wiser than we; for he says, 'With regard to the works of men, by the word of thy lips I have avoided the ways of the violent.' "[2]

They lay thus, bewailing themselves in the net. At last they spied a Shining One coming towards them with a whip of small cords in his hand. When he had reached the place where they were, he asked them whence they came and what they did there. They told him that they were poor Pilgrims going to Zion, but had been led out of their Way by a man clothed in white who bid them follow him, saying that he too was going to Mount Zion.

Then the Shining One said, "It is the Flatterer, a false apostle who has transformed himself into an angel of light."[3] So he rent the net and let the men out. Then he said to them, "Follow me, that I may set you in your way again." He led them back to the Way which they had left to follow the Flatterer.

"Where did you sleep last night?" asked the Shining One.

They said, "With the Shepherds, on the Delectable Mountains."

He asked them then if they had not received from those Shepherds a note of direction for the road.

They answered, "Yes."

"But did you," said he, "when you were at a standstill,

pluck out and read your note?''

They answered, ''No.''

He asked them, ''Why?''

They said, ''We forgot.''

He asked them, ''Did not the Shepherds bid you beware of the Flatterer?''

They answered, ''Yes, but we did not imagine that this fine-spoken man could have been he.''[4]

Then I saw in my dream that he commanded them to lie down; when they did this, he chastised them sorely with his whip, to teach them the good Way wherein they should walk; and as he chastised them, he said, ''As many as I love, I rebuke and chasten; be zealous therefore and repent.''[5] Having done this, he bid them go on their way, and take good care to heed the other directions of the Shepherds. So they thanked him for all his kindness, and went quietly along the right way, singing:

> *Come higher, you that walk along the Way*
> *See how the Pilgrims fare who go astray!*
> *When they good counsel lightly did forget*
> *They soon were caught within the Flatterer's net.*
> *God rescued them again, but yet you see,*
> *They're scourged as well. Let this your warning be!*

Now, after a while they saw afar off someone coming quietly and alone towards them. Christian said to his fellow, ''Yonder is a man with his back toward Zion, and he is coming to meet us.''

''I see him,'' said Hopeful. ''Let us be careful now, lest he should also prove to be a flatterer.''

The man drew nearer and nearer, and at last came up to

them. His name was Atheist, and he asked them whither they were going.

"We are going to Mount Zion," replied Christian.

Then Atheist fell into a very great laughter.

"What is the meaning of your laughter?" Christian asked.

"I laugh to see what ignorant persons you are," replied the

ATHEIST

other scornfully, "to take upon you so tedious a journey and are likely to have nothing but your travel for your pains."

"Why, man," asked Christian, "do you think we shall not be received?"

"Received!" His voice carried contempt as he spoke. "There is no such place as you dream of in all this world."

"But there is in the world to come," said Christian.

Atheist went on: "When I was at home in my own country, I heard as you now affirm, and from that hearing went out to see. I have been seeking this city for twenty years, but I find no more of it than I did the first day I set out."[6]

"But we have both heard and believe that there is such a place to be found," said Christian.

Atheist shook his head. "If I had not believed when at home, I would not have come this far to seek. But since I have found none (and certainly I should have if there is any such place to be found, for I have gone to seek it further than you), I am going back again and will seek to refresh myself with the things that I cast away then, for hopes of what I see now is not."

Then said Christian to Hopeful, his fellow, "Is it true, what this man has said?"

"Take heed!" said Hopeful. "He is one of the flatterers. Remember what it has cost us once already for listening to such kind of fellows. What? No Mount Zion? Did we not see from the Delectable Mountains the gate of the city? And are we not now to walk by faith? Let us go on," said Hopeful, "lest the man with the whip overtake us again.[7] You should have taught me this lesson, which I will now return to you: 'Cease, my son, to hear the instruction that causes you to err from the words of knowledge.'[8] I say, my brother, cease listening to him, and let us 'believe to the saving of the soul.' "[9]

Christian smiled at Hopeful. "I did not put the question to

you because I doubted the truth of our belief myself, but to prove you and to draw from you the fruit of the honesty of your heart. As for this man, I know that he is blinded by the god of this world. Let us go on, you and I, knowing that we have belief of the truth, and 'no lie is of the truth.' "[10]

Hopeful replied, "I rejoice in hope of the glory of God."

So they turned away from the man, and he, still laughing at them, went his way.

Notes on Chapter 18

[1] *Proverbs 29:5*

[2] *Psalm 17:4*

[3] *Daniel 11:32* He shall seduce with flattery those who violate the covenant, but the people who know their God shall stand firm and take action. *II Corinthians 11:13,14* For such men are false apostles, deceitful workmen, disguising themselves as apostles of Christ. And no wonder, for even Satan disguises himself as an angel of light.

[4] *Romans 16:18* For such persons do not serve our Lord Christ, but their own appetites, and by fair and flattering words they deceive the hearts of the simple-minded.

[5] *Revelation 3:19* Those whom I love, I reprove and chasten; so be zealous and repent.

[6] *Jeremiah 22:12* But in the place where they have carried him captive, there shall he die, and he shall never see this land again. *Ecclesiastes 10:15* The toil of a fool wearies him, so that he does not know the way to the city.

[7] *II Corinthians 5:7* For we walk by faith and not by sight.

[8] *Proverbs 19:27*

[9] *Hebrews 10:39* But we are not of those who shrink back and are destroyed, but of those who have faith and keep their souls.

[10] *I John 2:21*

19

Hopeful's Testimony

I saw then in my dream that they went on till they came to a certain country where the air naturally tended to make one drowsy as he came as a stranger into it. Here Hopeful began to be very dull and sleepy, and said to Christian, "I am beginning to grow so drowsy that I can scarcely hold up my eyelids. Let us lie down here and take a nap."

"By no means!" replied Christian sharply. "Lest sleeping we never wake again!"

"Why, my brother?" asked Hopeful. "Sleep is sweet to the laboring man. We may be refreshed if we take a nap."

Christian looked at him sternly. "Do you not remember that one of the Shepherds bid us beware of the Enchanted Ground? He meant by that that we should beware of sleeping. 'Therefore let us not sleep as do others, but let us watch and be sober.' "[1]

"I acknowledge myself in a fault," said Hopeful, smiling. "If I had been here alone, I would have, by sleeping, run the danger of death. I see what the wise man says is true, 'Two are better than one.' Hitherto your company has been my mercy, and you will have good reward for your labor."[2]

"Now then," said Christian, "to prevent drowsiness in this place, let us have a good talk."

"With all my heart," said the other.

"Where shall we begin?" he asked.

"Where God began with us," replied Hopeful. "But you begin, if you please."

Christian said, "First I will sing you a little song:

> *When saints do sleepy grow, let them come hither,*
> *And hear how these two Pilgrims talk together:*
> *Yea, let them learn from them, in any wise,*
> *Thus to keep open drowsy, slumb'ring eyes.*
> *Saints' fellowship, if it is managed well*
> *Keeps them awake, and that in spite of hell.*

Then Christian began, saying, "I will ask you a question. How did you come at first to think of doing as you do now?"

"Do you mean, how did I come at first to look after the good of my soul?" asked Hopeful.

"Yes," replied the other. "That is my meaning."

Hopeful began his story. "I continued a good while in the delight of those things which were seen and sold at our fair; things which I believe now would have, had I continued in them, drowned me in perdition and destruction."

"What things are you speaking of?" Christian interjected.

"All the treasures and riches of the world," answered Hopeful. "I delighted much in wild and boisterous behavior, partying, drinking, swearing, lying, immorality, Sabbath-breaking and what-not — all of which tended to destroy the soul. But I found at last, by hearing and considering things that are Divine, which I heard from you and from beloved Faithful who was put to death for his faith and good life in Vanity Fair, that 'the end of these things is death.'[3] And that for these things' sake 'comes the wrath of God on the children of disobedience.'"[4]

HOW FAITHFUL INSTRUCTED HOPEFUL

"And did you presently fall under the power of this conviction?" asked Christian again.

"No," was the answer, "I was not willing at once to know the evil of sin nor the damnation that follows upon the commission of it. I endeavored instead, when my mind at first began to be shaken with the Word, to shut my eyes against the light of it."

Christian asked, "But what was the cause of your resistance to the workings of God's blessed Spirit on you at the first?"

Hopeful said, "Well, first, I was ignorant that this was the working of God on me. I never thought that by awaking to the consciousness of sin that God at first begins the conversion of a sinner. Then, too, sin was still very sweet to my flesh, and I was loath to leave it. A third thing that held me back was that I did not know how to part from my old companions — their presence and actions were still so desirable to me. And finally, the hours in which convictions were on me were such troublesome and such heart-frightening hours that I could not bear so much as the remembrance of them on my heart.''

''Then, as it seems, sometimes you got rid of your trouble,'' observed his companion.

''Yes,'' he went on, ''I did indeed. But it would come into my mind again, and then I would be as bad — no, worse,— than I had been before.''

HOPEFUL'S SINS BROUGHT TO MIND

"Why was this?" Christian inquired. "What was it that brought your sins to mind again?"

"Many things," said Hopeful, remembering. "If I met a good man in the streets, or if I heard anyone read in the Bible, or if my head should begin to ache, I would remember. Or if I were told that some of my neighbors were sick, or if I heard the bell toll for someone who had died, or if the thought of dying myself should come to mind, I would remember my sins. If I heard that sudden death had happened to someone else, but especially, when I thought of myself, that I must quickly come to judgment, my sins accused me."

"Did you find that you could at any time with any ease, get rid of the guilt of your sin when by any of these ways the conviction of it came on you?" asked Christian.

"No, not I. I found that they got faster hold on my conscience and if I but thought of going back to sin, it would be double torment to me," said Hopeful.

"So what did you do then?" asked the other.

Hopeful said, "I decided I must try to amend my life. For else, thought I, I am sure to be damned!"

"And did you try to amend?" asked his friend.

"Oh, yes," said Hopeful. "I fled not only from my sins but from sinful company, too. I took up religious duties, such as prayer, reading, weeping for sin, speaking truth to my neighbors, and so on. I did these things, and too many others to mention here now."

"And did you think yourself to be well then?" asked Christian.

"Yes, for a while," Hopeful smiled as he spoke. "But, after a time, my trouble came tumbling on me again, and that in spite of all my reformations!"

"But how did that come about, since you were now reformed?" queried his companion.

Hopeful continued: "Well, there were several things that would bring this conviction back upon me, especially such sayings as these: 'All our righteousnesses are as filthy rags.'[5] 'By the works of the law shall no man be justified.'[6] 'When you have done all these things, say, We are unprofitable.'[7] And there were many more like these.

"I began to reason with myself like this: If *all* my righteousnesses are filthy rags; if by the deeds of the law *no* man can be justified; and if, when we have done *all*, we are yet unprofitable, then it is but a folly to think of heaven by the law. And then I thought like this: If a man runs a hundred pounds into debt to a shopkeeper, and after that shall pay for everything he buys, yet, if the old debt stands still on the books, for that the shopkeeper can sue him and throw him into prison until he shall pay the debt."

"Well, and how did you apply this to yourself?" was the next question.

"Why, I thought thus with myself: I have, by my sins, run up a great debt into God's book, and that by reforming now, I cannot pay that score. Therefore I should think still, in spite of all my amendments of life: but how shall I be freed from that damnation which I have brought myself in danger of by my former transgressions?"

"A very good application," said Christian. "But, pray, go on."

"Another thing that had troubled me since my tardy amendment of life was that if I look carefully into the best of what I did now, I still saw sin — new sin, mixing itself with the best of what I do. So now I was forced to conclude that, notwithstanding my former prideful thoughts concerning myself and my duties, I have committed sin enough in performing one duty to send me to hell, even if my former life had been faultless."[8]

Christian asked, "What did you do then?"

"Do! I could not tell what to do," exclaimed the other, "until I opened my mind to Faithful, for he and I became well acquainted. He told me that unless I could obtain the righteousness of a man who had never sinned, neither my own nor all the righteousness of the world could save me."

"And did you think he spoke the truth?"

Hopeful responded, "If he had told me so when I was pleased and satisfied with my own reformation, I would have called him a fool for his pains. But now that I had seen my own weakness and the sin that clings to my best performance, I was forced to agree with what he said."

"But did you think, when at first he suggested it to you, that there was such a man to be found, of whom it might justly be said, that he never committed sin?" asked Christian.

"I must confess," replied Hopeful, "that the words sounded strange at first; but after a little more talk and company with him I had full conviction about it."

"And did you ask him what man this was, and how you must be justified by him?"

"Yes, and he told me that it was the Lord Jesus, who dwells at the right hand of the Most High. He told me that I must be justified by Him even by trusting to what He has done by Himself in the days of His flesh, and what He suffered when He hung on the Cross. I asked him further how that man's righteousness could be of such efficacy to justify another before God. And he told me that He was the mighty God, and did what He did, and died the death also, not for Himself, but for me; and that His doings and the worthiness of them would be imputed to me if I believed on Him."[9]

Christian spoke again. "What did you do then?"

"I made my objections against my believing, for I thought He was not willing to save me," said Hopeful.

"And what did Faithful say to you then?"

"He bid me go to Him and see," said Hopeful, remembering. "Then I said this was presumption; but he said, no, for I was invited to come.[10] Then he gave me a Book of Jesus, His words, to encourage me the more freely to come; and he said, concerning that Book, that every jot and tittle of it stood firmer than heaven and earth.[11] Then I asked him, 'What must I do to come to Him?' And he told me I must entreat upon my knees, with all my heart and soul, 'Father, reveal Him to me.'[12] I asked him further how I must make my supplication to Him, and he said, 'Go, and you will find Him on a mercy-seat, where He sits all the year long, to give pardon and forgiveness to them who come.' I told him that I knew not what to say when I came. And he bid me say to this effect: 'God be merciful to me a sinner, and make me to know and believe in Jesus Christ; for I see that if His righteousness had not been, or if I do not have faith in that righteousness, I am utterly cast away. Lord, I have heard that Thou art a merciful God, and hast ordained that Thy Son Jesus Christ should be the Savior of the world; and that Thou art willing to bestow Him upon such a poor sinner as I am, and I am a sinner indeed! Lord, take therefore, this opportunity and magnify Thy grace in the salvation of my soul, through Thy Son Jesus Christ. Amen.' "[13]

"And did you do as you were bidden?" asked his companion.

"Yes," said Hopeful, "over and over and over."

"And did the Father reveal His Son to you?"

"Not at first, nor second, nor third, nor fourth, nor fifth — no, nor at the sixth time either!" said Hopeful.

"What did you do then?" Christian queried.

"Why, I could not tell what to do!" he exclaimed.

"Did you have thoughts of leaving off praying?" he asked again.

"Yes," was the reply, "an hundred times twice told. The reason I did not was that I believed that what had been told me was true; — that is, that without the righteousness of this Christ, all the world could not save me, and therefore I thought within myself, if I leave off I die, and I can but die at the throne of grace. So with all this came this thought into my mind, 'Though it tarry, wait for it; because it will surely come, it will not tarry.'[14] So I continued praying until the Father showed me His Son."

"How was He revealed to you?" asked Christian eagerly.

Hopeful continued: "I did not see Him with my bodily eyes, but with the eyes of my understanding.[15] It happened this way: one day I was very sad, I think sadder than at any one time in my life, and this sadness was through a fresh sight of the greatness and vileness of my sins. As I was then looking for nothing but hell and the everlasting damnation of my soul, suddenly, as I thought, I saw the Lord Jesus Christ look down from heaven upon me, and saying, 'Believe on the Lord Jesus Christ, and you will be saved.'[16]

"But I replied, 'Lord, I am a great, a very great sinner.' And He answered, 'My grace is sufficient for you.'[17] Then I said, 'But, Lord, what is believing?' And then I saw from that saying, 'He that comes to me shall never hunger, and he who believes on me shall never thirst,'[18] that believing and coming was all one; and that he who comes, that is, runs out in his heart and affections after salvation by Christ, he indeed believes in Christ. Then the tears stood in my eyes, and I asked further, 'But Lord, may such a great sinner as I am be indeed accepted of Thee, and be saved by Thee?' And I heard Him say, 'And him that comes to me I will in no wise cast out.'[19] Then I said, 'But Lord, how must I think of Thee in order that my faith may be placed aright on Thee?' And He said, 'Christ Jesus came into the world to save sinners.'[20] 'He is the end of the law for righteousness to everyone who believes.'[21] 'He died for our sins, and rose again for our justification.'[22] 'He loved us, and washed us from our sins in His own blood.'[23] 'He is mediator between God and us.'[24] 'He ever lives to make intercession for us.'[25] From all these I gathered that I must look for righteousness in His person, and for satisfaction for my sins by His blood; that what He did in obedience to His Father's law, and in submitting to the penalty of it, was not for Himself but for those who will accept it for their salvation and be thankful. And now my heart was full of joy, my eyes filled with tears, and my affections were running over with love to the name, the people and the ways of Jesus Christ.''

''This was a revelation of Christ to your soul indeed,'' said his brother. ''But tell me particularly what effect this had upon your spirit.''

Hopeful said, ''It made me see that all the world, in spite of all the righteousness of it, is in a state of condemnation. It made me see that God the Father, though he is just, can justly justify the repentant sinner. It made me greatly ashamed of the vileness of my former life, and confounded me with the sense of my own ignorance. For there never came any thought into my heart before now that had so shown me the beauty of Jesus Christ. It made me love a holy life, and long to do something for the honor and glory of the name of the Lord Jesus; yes, I thought that had I now a thousand gallons of blood in my body, I could spill it all for the sake of the Lord Jesus.''

Notes on Chapter 19

[1] *I Thessalonians 5:6*

[2] *Ecclesiastes 4:9, 10a* Two are better than one, because they will have a good reward for their toil. For if they fall, one will lift up his fellow.

[3] *Romans 6:21-23* But then what return did you get from the things of which you are now ashamed? The end of those things is death. But now that you

have been set free from sin and have become slaves of God, the return you get is sanctification and its end, eternal life. For the wages of sin is death, but the free gift of God is eternal life in Christ Jesus our Lord.

[4]*Ephesians 5:6*

[5]*Isaiah 64:6*

[6]*Galatians 2:16*

[7]*Luke 17:10*

[8]This is one of the most important and hardest-to-learn truths of the Christian life. It cuts across all easy self-righteousness and self-praise, and goes to the very heart of the great central truth that it is through grace that we are saved, not by works, lest any man should boast. *(Ephesians 2:8)* In another place, Bunyan says, "For there is not a day, nor a duty; not a day that thou livest nor a duty that thou dost, but will need that mercy should come after to take away thy iniquity." *Ed.*

[9]*Hebrews 10, Romans 4, Colossians 1, I Peter 1.*

[10]*Matthew 24:35* Come to me, all who labor and are heavy laden, and I will give you rest.

[11]*Matthew 24:25* Heaven and earth will pass away, but my words will not pass away.

[12]*Psalm 95:6* O come, let us worship and bow down, let us kneel before the Lord our Maker! *Daniel 6:10b* . . . And he go down on his knees three times a day and prayed and gave thanks before his God, as he had done previously. *Jeremiah 29:12,13* Then you will call upon me and come and pray to me, and I will hear you. You will seek me and find me; when you seek me with all your heart.

[13]*Exodus 25:22* There I will meet with you and from above the mercy seat, from between the two cherubim that are upon the ark of the testimony, I will speak with you of all that I will give you in commandment for the people of Israel. *Leviticus 16:2b* . . . For I will appear in the cloud upon the mercy seat. *Numbers 7:89* And when Moses went into the tent of meeting to speak with the Lord, he heard the voice speaking to him from above the mercy seat that was upon the ark of the testimony, from between the cherubim; and it spoke to him. *Hebrews 4:16* Let us then with confidence draw near to the throne of grace, that we may receive mercy and find grace to help in time of need.

[14]*Habakkuk 2:3*

[15]*Ephesians 1:18,19* Having the eyes of your hearts enlightened, that you may know what is the hope to which he has called you, what are the riches of his glorious inheritance in the saints, and what is the immeasurable

greatness of his power in us who believe, according to the working of his great might.

[16] *Acts 16:31*

[17] *II Corinthians 12:9*

[18] *John 6:35*

[19] *John 6:37*

[20] *I Timothy 1:15*

[21] *Romans 10:4*

[22] *Romans 4:25*

[23] *Revelation 1:5*

[24] *I Timothy 2:5*

[25] *Hebrews 7:25*

20

Christian Talks with Ignorance

 saw then in my dream that Hopeful looked back and saw Ignorance, whom they had left far behind, coming along after them.

"Look," said he to Christian, "how far that young man loiters behind us."

"Yes, yes, I see him," said Christian. "He doesn't care for our company."

"But I suppose it would not have hurt him if he had kept pace with us," observed Hopeful.

"True," said his friend, "but I warrant you he thinks otherwise."

"I think he does," said Hopeful, "but let's wait for him." So they did. Then Christian said to Ignorance, "Come on, man. Why do you stay so behind?"

Ignorance replied, "I take my pleasure in walking alone a great deal more than in company unless I like the company better."

Then said Christian to Hopeful, under his breath, "Did I not tell you that he cared not for our company?" To Ignorance he spake: "Come up, and let us talk away the time in this lonely place. Come, how is it with you? How does it stand between God and your soul now?"

"I hope well," replied the other. "For I am always full of good thoughts that come into my mind to comfort me as I walk."

"What good thoughts? Pray tell us," said Christian.

"Why, I think of God and heaven," said Ignorance.

"So do the devils and damned souls," returned Christian.

"But I think of them, and desire them," said Ignorance again.

"So do many that are never likely to come there," said Christian. "The soul of the sluggard craves, and gets nothing."[1]

Ignorance would not be put off. "But I think of them and leave all for them."

Christian shook his head. "That I doubt; for leaving all is a hard matter. Yes, a harder matter than many are aware of. But why, or by what, are you persuaded that you have left all for God and heaven?"

"My heart tells me so," replied Ignorance.

Christian shook his head again. "The wise man says, 'He that trusts in his own heart is a fool.' "[2]

"This is speaking of an evil heart, but mine is a good one," said Ignorance.

"But how do you prove that?" asked Christian.

"It comforts me in hopes of heaven," was the reply.

"That may be, through its deceitfulness; for a man's heart may minister comfort to him in the hopes of that thing for which he yet has no ground to hope," Christian went on.

"But my heart and life agree together, and therefore my hope is well grounded," answered Ignorance confidently.

"Who told you that your heart and life agree together?" asked Christian.

"My heart tells me so," replied Ignorance.

Christian exclaimed, "Your heart tells you so! Except the Word of God bears witness in this matter, no other testimony is of any value."

Ignorance asked, "But is it not a good heart which has good thoughts? And is not that a good life that is according to God's commandments?"

"Yes," replied the other, "that is a good heart that has good thoughts and that is a good life that is lived according to God's commandments. But it is one thing indeed to *have* these, and another thing only to *think* so."

"Well," said Ignorance, "do tell me what you count good thoughts and a life according to God's commandments."

"There are good thoughts of various kinds," said Christian. "Some concerning ourselves, some concerning God, some Christ, and some other things. Good thoughts concerning ourselves are those which agree with the Word of God."

"And when do our thoughts of ourselves agree with the Word of God?" he asked.

Christian said, "When we pass the same judgment upon ourselves which the Word passes. To explain myself — the Word of God says of persons in a natural condition, 'There is none righteous, there is none that doeth good.'³ It also says that every imagination of the heart of man is only evil, and that continually.⁴ And again, 'The imagination of man's heart is evil from his youth.'⁵ Now then, when we think thus of ourselves, having this realization of it, then our thoughts are good ones, because they are according to the Word of God."

"I will never believe that my heart is so bad," said Ignorance.

Christian went on, "For this reason you have never had one good thought concerning yourself in your life! But let me go on. As the Word passes a judgment on our *heart*, so it passes judgment on our *ways,* and when the thoughts of our hearts and ways agree with the judgment which the Word gives of both, then both are good, because they agree with the Word.''

''Please make your meaning a little clearer,'' said Ignorance.

''Why, the Word of God says that man's ways are crooked ways — not good, but perverse,''[6] said the other. ''It says they are naturally out of the good way, that they have not known it.[7] Now, when a man thinks thus of his ways — when he feels and with humiliation of heart thinks like this, then he has good thoughts of his own ways, because his thoughts now agree with the judgment of the Word of God.''

''What are good thoughts concerning God?'' asked Ignorance, not desiring to prolong the talk of the heart and ways of man.

''Even as I said concerning our thoughts about ourselves, when our thoughts of God agree with what the Word says of Him: and that is, when we think of His being and attributes as the Word has taught — but I cannot talk of these at large now. But to speak of Him with reference to us, to think that He knows us better than we know ourselves, and can see sin in us when and where we can see none in ourselves. When we think He knows our inmost thought and that our heart, with all its depths, is always open to His eyes. Also when we think that all our righteousness stinks in His nostrils, and that He cannot abide seeing us standing before Him in any self-confidence, even in all our best performances.''

Ignorance was getting angry. ''Do you think that I am such a fool as to think God can see no further than I? or, that I would come to God in the best of my performances?''

''Why, how do you think in this matter?'' asked Christian.

''To be brief,'' said Ignorance, ''I think I must believe in Christ for justification.''

"How!" exclaimed Christian. "You think you must believe in Christ but do not see your need of Him! You neither see your original nor actual weaknesses, but have such an opinion of yourself and of what you do that it is plain to see you never saw any necessity of Christ's personal righteousness to justify you before God! How do you say then, 'I believe in Christ'?"

"I believe well enough for all that!" Ignorance retorted.

"How do you believe?" asked Christian.

Ignorance replied, "I believe that Christ died for sinners, and that I shall be justified before God from the curse through His gracious acceptance of my obedience to His law. Or in this way: Christ makes my duties that are religious acceptable to His Father by virtue of His merits, and so I shall be justified."

"Let me give an answer to this confession of your faith," said Christian. "First, you believe with a *fantastical* faith, because this faith is nowhere described in the Word. It is the product of your own fantasy.

"Second, you believe with a *false* faith, because your faith takes justification away from the personal righteousness of Jesus Christ, and applies it to your own righteousness.

"Third, your faith does not make Christ a justifier of your person, but of your actions, and of your soul because of your right actions, which is false.

"Fourth, this faith is deceitful, and will leave you under wrath in the day of God Almighty. For true, justifying faith puts the soul, painfully conscious of its lost condition by the Law, fleeing for refuge to Christ's righteousness, which is His personal obedience to the law in doing and suffering for us what is required at our hands. This righteousness, I say, true faith accepts as covering the soul and by it the soul is presented as spotless before God, accepted and acquitted from condemnation."

"What!" exclaimed Ignorance again. "Would you have us trust to what Christ in His own person has done without us? This opinion of yours would loosen the reins of our lust and allow us to live any way we please. What matter would it be how we lived, if we may be justified by Christ's personal righteousness from all, when we believe it?"

"Ignorance is your name," said Christian sadly. "And as your name, so are you. Even this your answer demonstrates what I say. You are ignorant of what justifying righteousness is, and just as ignorant of how to secure your soul through faith in it from the heavy wrath of God. Yes, and you are also ignorant of the true effects of saving faith in this righteousness of Christ, which is to bow and win over the heart of God in Christ, to love His name, His word, ways and people, — not as you ignorantly imagine!"

Hopeful interjected: "Ask him if he ever had Christ revealed to him from heaven."

"What! You are a man for revelations!" Ignorance sneered. "I believe that what both of you and all your kind say about this matter is but the fruit of distracted brains."

"Why, man!" said Hopeful, "Christ is so hidden in God from our natural apprehensions of the flesh that no man can savingly know Him unless God the Father reveals Him to him."

"That is your faith, but not mine," returned the other. "Yet mine, I have no doubt, is as good as yours, though I have not got so many whimsies in my head as you."

"Allow me to put in a word," said Christian gravely. "You ought not so slightly to talk of this matter. For I will boldly affirm what my good companion has just said: that no man can know Jesus Christ but by the revelation of the Father.[8] Yes, and faith, too, by which the soul lays hold on Christ, must be wrought by the exceeding greatness of His mighty power; the working of which faith, I perceive, poor Ignorance, you are ignorant of.[9] Be awakened then; see your own wretchedness, and flee to the Lord Jesus; and by His righteousness, which is the righteousness of God (for He Himself is God), you shall be delivered from condemnation.''

Ignorance said, "You go so fast I cannot keep up your pace. Do go on before; I must stay awhile behind.''

Then Christian said to Hopeful, "Well, come my good Hopeful, I perceive that we must walk by ourselves again.''

Notes on Chapter 20

[1] *Proverbs 13:4*

[2] *Proverbs 28:26*

[3] *Romans 3:10,12*

[4] *Genesis 6:5*

[5] *Genesis 8:21*

[6] *Psalm 125:5, Proverbs 2:15*

[7] *Romans 3:17* And the way of peace they do not know.

[8] *Matthew 11:27* All things have been delivered to me by my Father, and no one knows the Son except the Father, and no one knows the Father except the Son and anyone to whom the Son chooses to reveal him.

Therefore I want you to understand that no one speaking by the Spirit of God ever says "Jesus be cursed!" and no one can say "Jesus is Lord!" except by the Holy Spirit.

[9] *Ephesians 1:18,19* Having the eyes of your hearts enlightened that you may know what is the hope to which he has called you, what are the riches of his glorious inheritance in the saints, and what is the immeasurable greatness of his power in us who believe, according to the working of his great might.

21

To the Land of Beulah

I saw in my dream that Christian and Hopeful went on ahead, and Ignorance came hobbling after.

Christian said to his companion, "I feel very sorry for this poor man, for it will certainly go ill with him at last."

"Alas!" replied Hopeful, "there are many others in our town in his condition — whole families, whole streets, even of pilgrims too. And if there are so many in our area, how many do you think there must be in the place where Ignorance was born?"

"Indeed, the Word says, 'He had blinded their eyes, lest they should see.'[1] But now that we are alone, what do you think of such men? Have they at no time, do you think, any conviction of sin, and are they never afraid that their state is a dangerous one?" asked Christian.

"I'll let you answer that one," replied Hopeful, smiling, "for you are older than I."

Christian continued: "Then I say, I think they may sometimes have such convictions and fears. But, being naturally ignorant, they do not understand that such convictions are for their good; so they desperately seek to stifle them and they presumptuously continue to flatter themselves in the way of their own hearts.''

Hopeful nodded. ''I do believe, as you say, that fear tends much to men's good, and helps to set them right, especially at the very beginning of their pilgrimage.''

''Without all doubt it does, if it is right fear. 'The fear of the Lord is the beginning of wisdom,' ''[2] said Christian.

''How would you describe what you call 'right fear'?'' asked Hopeful.

Christian replied, ''True or right fear can be identified three ways: by its beginning — it is caused by conviction of sin; and it drives the soul to lay fast hold on Christ for salvation; and it begets and nourishes in the soul a great reverence for God, for His Word and ways, keeping the heart tender and making it afraid to turn from them to the right hand or to the left, to anything that would dishonor God, break the peace of the soul, grieve the Spirit, or cause the enemy to speak reproachfully.''

''Well said,'' replied his friend. ''I believe you have said the truth. Are we now almost out of Enchanted Ground?''

''Why,'' Christian asked, ''are you weary of this line of talk?''

''Not at all,'' replied Hopeful. ''It is only that I would like to know where we are.''

''We have not more than two miles farther to go on Enchanted Ground,'' said Christian. ''But let us return to our subject. Now the ignorant do not know that such convictions as tend to put them in fear are for their good, and therefore they seek to stifle them.''

''How do they do this?'' asked the other.

''Well,'' said Christian, ''they think that those fears come from the devil, when in actuality they come from God. Thinking so, they resist them as things that would hurt or destroy them. They also think that these fears spoil their faith, when alas for them, poor men that they are, they have none at all! So they harden their hearts against them. Then they presume they ought not to fear, and, in spite of them, grow presumptuous and over-confident. They see that those fears tend to take away from them their pitiful old self-holiness and so they resist them with all their might.''

"I know something of that myself," said Hopeful. "It was that way with me before I knew myself."

"Well, we will leave at this time our neighbor Ignorance and take up another profitable question," said his friend.

Hopeful smiled at Christian, "Gladly, but you must still begin."

Christian began: "Did you know about ten years ago, one Temporary in your part of the country, who was very prominent in religion then?"

"Know him!" exclaimed Hopeful. "Yes, he dwelt in Graceless, a town about two miles from Honest, and he lived next door to a fellow named Turnback."

"Right; he lived under the same roof with him," said Christian. "Well that man was much awakened once, I believe, and he then had some sight of his sins and the wages that they would bring."

"I agree with you," said Hopeful. "My house is not more than three miles from his, and he would often come to me and talk with many tears. Truly I pitied the man, and was not without hope for him. But one may see it is not every one who cries, 'Lord, Lord.' ''

"He told me once that he was resolved to go on pilgrimage as we go now," said the other, "but all of a sudden he became acquainted with a man named Save-self, and then he became a stranger to me."

"Since you mentioned him, let us think a little about the reason for the sudden backsliding of people like him," suggested Hopeful.

"That might be very good. But in this case, I insist that you begin."

Hopeful spoke without hesitation. "Well then, there are in my judgment, four reasons for such backsliding.

"First, though the consciences of such men are awakened, yet their minds are not changed. Thus, when the power of guilt wears away, what provoked them to be religious ceases, and they naturally turn to their own course again.[3] Since they were eager for heaven only because of a fear of the torments of hell, as soon as that fear subsides, their desire for salvation and heaven also subsides. So it comes to pass that when their guilt and fear are gone, their desire for heaven and happiness dies, and they return to their old course again.

"Another reason is that they have slavish fears that over-master them. I am speaking now of the fears they have of men, for 'the fear of man bringeth a snare.'[4] So then, though they may seem to be eager for heaven as long as the flames of hell are about their ears, yet when that terror has subsided a little, they have second thoughts — namely, that it is good to be wise and not to run the hazard of losing everything for something they do not know, or at least, of bringing themselves into unavoidable and unnecessary troubles. And so, they fall in with the world again.

"The embarrassment that attends open profession of Christ is also a block in their way. They are proud and haughty, and religion in their eye is low and contemptible. So, when they have lost their fear of hell and the wrath to come, they return again to their old life.

"They cannot bear to look at their guilt or think of the terror that is before them. They prefer to postpone thinking about it, though, perhaps if they were willing, it would make them flee to where the righteous flee and there be safe, that is to Jesus Christ. But because they shun even the thought of guilt and terror, once they are rid of their awakenings about the wrath of God, they harden their hearts gladly and quickly, and choose such ways as will harden them more and more.''

"You are pretty close to the truth of it," said Christian "For the bottom of it all is an unchanged mind and will. Therefore they are like the criminal who stands before the judge and trembles. He seems to repent most heartily, but the bottom of all is the fear of prison. It is not that he has any hatred of his crime, as is proved when the man is free and steals again — so a criminal still. But, if his mind was changed, he would be otherwise.''

Hopeful responded, "Now that I have shown you the reasons why they backslide, will you talk about the manner of backsliding?''

Said Christian, "So I will, willingly. First, they draw off as many of their own thoughts as possible away from any remembrance of God, of death, or of the judgment to come. That is the first step. Then they cast off by degrees their private duties of the inner life — secret prayer, curbing their lusts, watching, sorrow for sin, and the like. Then they shun the company of lively and warm Christians. After that, they grow cold to their public duty — such as hearing and reading the Word, seeking godly counsel, and the like. Then they begin to pick holes, as we say, in some of the godly — to find fault with them, so that they may have a respectable reason for deserting their own former walk of life. Then they begin to cling to and associate themselves with carnal, loose and wanton persons. Then they give way to carnal and wanton talk, jokes, stories and tidbits of gossip. They are especially glad if they can do this with some who are counted honest, that they may be made more bold by their example. After this, they begin to play with little sins openly. And then, being hardened, they show themselves as they are. Thus, being launched again into the gulf of misery, unless a miracle of grace stop it, they everlastingly perish in their own deceptions.''

By this time the Pilgrims had gotten over the Enchanted Ground, and were entering into the country of Beulah, whose air was very sweet and pleasant. Since their way led directly through it, they were able to solace themselves there for a time.[5] Yes, here they heard continually the singing of birds, and saw every day the flowers appear in the earth, and heard the voice of the turtle-dove in the land.[6] In this country the sun shines night and day, being beyond the Valley of the Shadow of Death. It was out of reach of Giant Despair, so that they could not so much as see Doubting Castle from this land. Here they were within sight of the city to which they were going, and here there met them some of its inhabitants, for in this land the Shining Ones commonly walked, because it was upon the borders of heaven.

In this land, also, the contract between the bride and Bridegroom was renewed — "As the bridegroom rejoices over the bride, so did their God rejoice over them.''[7] Here they had no lack of grain and wine, for in this place they met with abundance of what they had sought in all their pilgrimage. Here all the inhabitants of the country called them "the holy people,'' "the redeemed of the Lord,'' and "sought out.''

Now, as they walked in this land, they had more rejoicing than they had had when they were further away from the Kingdom to which they were bound. Drawing near to the city, they had a more perfect view of it. It was built of pearls and precious stones, and the street of it was paved with gold, so that by the natural glory of the city and the reflection of the sunbeams on it, Christian fell sick with desire for it. Hopeful, too, had an attack of sickness once or twice. So there they lay for a while, crying out, because of their pangs, "If you find my Beloved, tell Him that I am sick of love.''[8]

THE PILGRIMS IN SIGHT OF THE HOLY CITY

But, being strengthened a little, and better able to bear their sickness, they walked on their way, and came nearer and nearer to it. There they found orchards, vineyards and gardens, whose gates opened into the highway. As they came up to these places, the gardener stood in the road, and the Pilgrims asked, ''Whose goodly vineyards and gardens are these?'' He answered, ''They are the King's, and are planted here for His own delight and for the help of pilgrims.'' So they were invited into the vineyards and told to refresh themselves and eat their fill.[9] The gardener also showed them the King's walks, and the arbors where He delighted to be; and here they tarried and slept.

Now I beheld in my dream, that they talked more in their sleep at this period than they had ever done in all their journey.

I wondered at this, but the gardener said to me, "Why do you wonder at the matter? It is the nature of the fruit of the grapes of these vineyards to go down so sweetly as to cause the lips of them that are asleep to speak."

When they awoke, they prepared themselves to go up to the City. But, as I said, the reflection of the sun upon the City was so extremely glorious that they could not, as yet, with open face behold it, (for "the city was pure gold"), so they had to look through an instrument made for that purpose.[10] I saw that as they went on, there met them two men in raiment that shone like gold, and whose faces shone as the light.

These men asked the Pilgrims whence they came, and they told them. They also asked them where they had lodged, and what difficulties and dangers, what comforts and pleasures they had met in the Way, and they told them.

Then said the men that met them, "You have but two difficulties more to meet with, and then you will be in the City."

Christian then, and his companion, asked the men to go along with them, and the men agreed to do this. "But," said they, "you must obtain it by your own faith."

So I saw in my dream that they went on together until they came in sight of the gate.

Notes on Chapter 21

[1] *John 12:40*

[2] *Proverbs 1:7, 9:10; Psalm 111:10* and *Job 28:28*

[3] *II Peter 2:22* It has happened to them according to the true proverb, The dog turns back to his own vomit, and the sow is washed only to wallow in the mire.

[4] *Proverbs 29:25* The fear of man lays a snare, but he who trusts in the Lord is safe.

[5] *Isaiah 62:4* Thou shalt no more be termed Forsaken; neither shall thy land any more be termed Desolate: but thou shalt be called Hephzibah, and thy land Beulah: for the Lord delighteth in thee, and thy land shall be married. (KJV)

[6]*Song of Solomon 2:10-12*

[7]*Isaiah 62:5,8,11 and 12*

[8]*Song of Solomon 5:8*

[9]*Deuteronomy 23:24*

[10]*II Corinthians 3:18* And we all, with unveiled face, beholding the glory of the Lord, are being changed into his likeness from one degree of glory to another; for this comes from the Lord who is the Spirit.

22

The Final Conflict

ow I saw that between the Pilgrims and the gate to the Celestial City lay a River, but there was no bridge to go over, and the River was very deep. At the sight of it, the Pilgrims were stunned, but the men who went with them said, "You must go through, or you cannot come to the gate."

The Pilgrims then began to inquire if there was no other way to the gate, to which the men answered, "Yes, but only two, Enoch and Elijah, have been permitted to tread that path since the foundation of the world, and no others will until the last trumpet shall sound."[1] The Pilgrims then, especially Christian, began to worry in their minds, and they looked this way and that, but no way could be found by which they might escape the River. Then they asked the men if the waters were all of the same depth. They said, "No," yet they could not help them in that case. "For," said they, "you shall find it deeper or more shallow as you believe in the King of the place."

The Pilgrims then addressed themselves to the water, and entering it, Christian began to sink. Crying out to his good friend, Hopeful, he said, "I sink in the deep waters; the billows go over my head; all his waves go over me!''

Then said Hopeful, ''Be of good cheer, my brother. I feel the bottom and it is good!''

Then said Christian, ''Ah! my friend, 'the sorrows of death have compassed me about'; I shall not see the land that flows with milk and honey.''

With that a great darkness and horror fell upon Christian, so he could not see before him. Here he also in great measure lost his senses, so that he could neither remember nor talk in an orderly way of those sweet refreshments that he had met with in the way of his pilgrimage. But all the words that he spoke still disclosed that he had horror of mind and heart that he would die in that River and never obtain entrance at the gate.

THE PILGRIMS CROSS THE RIVER OF DEATH.

Here, also, as they that stood by him perceived, he was much troubled at thoughts of the sins that he had committed, both before and after he became a Pilgrim. It was observed that he was troubled with apparitions of hobgoblins and evil spirits, because every now and then he would indicate that by what he said. Hopeful therefore had much to do to keep his brother's head above water. In fact, sometimes he would be quite out of sight, and then he would rise up again half dead. Hopeful also would try to comfort him, saying, "Brother, I see the gate and men standing by to receive us"; but Christian would answer, "It is you, it is you they wait for. You have been Hopeful ever since I knew you."

"And so have you," said the other.

"Ah, brother!" said Christian, "surely if I was right He would now arise and help me; but for my sins He has brought me into the snare and left me."

Then said Hopeful, "My brother, you have quite forgotten the text where it is said of the wicked, 'There are no bands in their death, but their strength is firm. They are not in trouble as other men, neither are they plagued like other men.'[2] These troubles and distresses that you are going through in these waters are no sign that God has forsaken you. They are sent to try you, whether you will call to mind what you have received beforehand of His goodness, and live upon Him in your distresses."

Then I saw in my dream that Christian was as though lost in thought for a while. Then Hopeful added this word, "Be of good cheer. Jesus Christ makes you whole!" With that Christian spoke out with a loud voice, "Oh, I see Him again! and He tells me, 'When thou passest through the waters, I will be with thee; and through the rivers, they shall not overflow thee.' "[3]

Then they both took courage, and the enemy was after that as still as a stone, until they had gotten across. Christian presently found ground to stand on, and so it followed that the rest of the River was but shallow. Thus they got over.

Now upon the bank of the River, on the other side, they saw the two Shining Men again, who were waiting for them there. As the Pilgrims came out of the River, the Men said to them, ''We are ministering spirits, sent forth to minister to them who shall be heirs of salvation.''[4] And so they went along towards the gate.

Now you must note that the City stood upon a mighty hill, but the Pilgrims went up that hill with ease, because they had these two men to lead them up by the arms. Also, they had left their mortal garments behind them in the River, for though they went in with them, they came out without them. Therefore they went up with much agility and speed, though the foundation upon which the City was placed was higher than the clouds. They therefore went up through the regions of the air, sweetly talking as they went, and much comforted because they had arrived safely over the River, and because they had such glorious companions to attend them.

The talk they had with the Shining Ones was about the glory of the place. They told them that the beauty and glory of the City was inexpressible. ''There,'' said they, ''is Mount Zion, the heavenly Jerusalem, the innumerable company of angels, and the spirits of just men made perfect.[5] You are going now to the paradise of God, in which you will see the Tree of Life, and eat of its never-fading fruits. When you come there, you will have white robes given you, and your walk and talk shall be every day with the King, even all the days of eternity.[6] There you shall not see again such things as you saw when you were in the lower region on the earth — sorrow, sickness, affliction and death, 'for the former things are passed away.' You are going to Abraham, to Isaac and Jacob and to the prophets — men that God has taken away from the evil to come, and who are now resting on their beds, each one walking in his uprightness.''[7]

THE PILGRIMS ASCEND THE HILL ESCORTED BY
THE HOST OF HEAVEN.

"What must we do in the holy place?" asked the Pilgrims.

The answer came, "You must there receive the comforts
of all your toil and have joy for all your sorrow; you must reap
what you have sown, even the fruit of all your prayers and
tears and sufferings for the King throughout your pilgrimage.[8]
In that place you must wear crowns of gold, and enjoy the
perpetual sight and vision of the Holy One, for 'there you shall

see Him as He is.'[9] There also you shall serve Him continually with praise, with shouting and thanksgiving, Whom you desired to serve in the world, though with much difficulty, because of the infirmity of your flesh. There your eyes shall be delighted with seeing and your ears with hearing the pleasant voice of the Mighty One. There you shall enjoy your friends again that have gone on before you. And there you shall with joy receive everyone who follows into the holy place after you. There also shall you be clothed with glory and majesty and put into a chariot fit to ride out with the King of Glory. When He shall come with sound of trumpet in the clouds, as upon the wings of the wind, you will come with Him. When he shall sit on the throne of judgment, you shall sit by Him. Yes, and when He shall pass sentence upon all the workers of iniquity, let them be angels or men, you also shall have a voice in that judgment, because they were His and your enemies.[10] Also, when He shall again return to the City, you shall go, too, with sound of trumpet, and be ever with Him."

Now, while they were thus drawing towards the gate, behold a company of the heavenly host came out to meet them. To the company, the two Shining Ones said, "These are the men who have loved our Lord when they were in the world and who left all for His holy name. He sent us to bring them and we have brought them thus far on their desired journey, that they may go in and look their Redeemer in the face with joy."

Then the heavenly host gave a great shout, saying, "Blessed are they which are called to the marriage supper of the Lamb." There came out also at this time to meet them several of the King's trumpeters dressed in white and shining clothing. They made the heavens echo with their loud and melodious sounds. These trumpeters saluted Christian and Hopeful with ten thousand welcomes from the world; and this they did with shouting and sound of trumpet.

Then they surrounded the Pilgrims on all sides. Some went before them, some behind, some on the right hand, some on the left, as if to guard them through the upper regions. And as they went they made the heavens resound with melodious music. It looked as though heaven itself was come down to meet them. Thus, therefore, they walked on together, and as they walked, the trumpeters continued their music, while with gestures of welcome and singing the host made them to know how glad they were to have them in their company and with what joy they had come out to meet them.

For the two Pilgrims, it was as though they were in heaven before they came to the gate, so swallowed up they were with the sight of the angels and the singing of the heavenly host. Here, too, they had the City itself in view, and they thought they heard all the bells in it ringing to welcome them to it. But above all, the warm and joyful thought they had about their own dwelling there with such a company as this — and that for ever and ever. Oh, by what tongue or pen can their glorious joy be expressed! And thus they came up to the gate.

Now when they had arrived at the gate of the City, there were written over it in letters of gold, "Blessed are they that do His commandments, that they may have right to the Tree of Life and may enter in through the gates into the City."[11]

Then I saw in my dream that the Shining Men told them to call at the gate, which they did. Some came and looked over the gate at them, namely, Enoch, Moses and Elijah and several others. It was said to them, "These Pilgrims have come from the City of Destruction for the love that they bear to the King of this place." Then each of the Pilgrims gave over his certificate which he had received at the beginning of his journey. Those, then, were carried in to the King, who when He had read them said, "Where are the men?"

"They are standing outside the gate," was the answer.

The King then commanded them to open the gate, "that

the righteous nation,'' said He, ''which keepeth the truth may enter in.''[12]

Now I saw in my dream that these two men went in at the gate: and lo! as they entered, they were transfigured, and they had raiment put on them that shone like gold. They also received harps and crowns — the harps to praise continually, and the crowns in token of honor.

Then I heard in my dream that all the bells in the City rang again for joy, and that it was said to the Pilgrims:

ENTER INTO THE JOY OF YOUR LORD.[13]

I also heard the men themselves, singing with a loud voice, saying,

BLESSING AND HONOR AND GLORY AND POWER BE UNTO HIM THAT SITTETH UPON THE THRONE AND UNTO THE LAMB FOR EVER AND EVER.[14]

Now just as the gates were opened to let in the men, I looked in after them, and behold the City shone like the sun; the streets also were paved with gold, and in the streets walked many men with crowns on their heads, palms in their hands, and golden harps for singing praises.

Some I saw had wings, and they answered one another without intermission, saying, ''Holy, holy, holy is the Lord.''[15] And after that, they shut up the gates, which when I had seen, I wished myself among them.

Notes on Chapter 22

[1] *I Corinthians 15:51,52* Lo! I tell you a mystery. We shall not all sleep, but we shall all be changed, in a moment, in the twinkling of an eye, at the

last trumpet. For the trumpet will sound, and the dead will be raised imperishable, and we shall be changed.

[2]*Psalm 73:4,5*

[3]*Isaiah 43:2*

[4]*Hebrews 1:14*

[5]*Hebrews 12:22-24*

[6]*Revelation 2:7b* To him who conquers I will grant to eat of the tree of life which is in the paradise of God. *Revelation 3:4b* They shall walk with me in white, for they are worthy. *Revelation 22:5* And night shall be no more; they need no light of lamp or sun, for the Lord God will be their light, and they shall reign for ever and ever.

[7]*Isaiah 57:1,2* The righteous man perishes, and no one lays it to heart; devout men are taken away, while no one understands. For the righteous man is taken away from calamity, he enters into peace; they rest in their beds who walk in their uprightness.

[8]*Galatians 6:7* Do not be deceived; God is not mocked, for whatever a man sows, that he will also reap.

[9]*I John 3:2*

[10]*I Thessalonians 4:13-17; Jude 14; Daniel 7:9,10; I Corinthians 6:2,3*

[11]*Revelation 22:14,15* Blessed are those who wash their robes, that they may have the right to the tree of life and that they may enter the city by the gates. Outside are the dogs and sorcerers and fornicators and murderers and idolaters, and every one who loves and practices falsehood.

[12]*Isaiah 26:2*

[13]*Matthew 25:21,23*

[14]*Revelation 5:13*

[15]*Isaiah 6:3*

23
A Concluding Warning

Now, while I was gazing on all these things, I turned my head to look back, and saw Ignorance coming up to the River side. But he soon got over, and that without half the difficulty which the other two Pilgrims had met with. For it happened that there was then in that place one Vain-hope, a ferryman, who with his boat helped him over. So he, as the others I had seen, ascended the hill to come up to the gate. But he came alone, and no man met him with the least encouragement. When he had arrived at the gate, he looked up to the writing that was above, and then began to knock, supposing that entrance would quickly be given to him. But he was asked by the men who looked over the top of the gate, "Where did you come from and what do you seek?"

He answered, "I have eaten and drunk in the presence of the King, and He has taught in our streets."[1]

Then they asked him for his certificate, that they might go in and show it to the King; so he fumbled in his bosom for one, but found none.

Then they said, "Have you no certificate?"

But the man answered never a word.

IGNORANCE THRUST INTO HELL

So they told the King, but He would not come down to see him. Instead, he commanded the two Shining Ones who had conducted Christian and Hopeful to the City to go out and take Ignorance, and bind him hand and foot, and have him away. Then they took him up, and carried him through the air, to the door that I saw in the side of the hill, and put him in there.

Then I saw that there was a way to hell, even from the gates of Heaven, as well as from the City of Destruction!

So I awoke, and behold it was a dream.

Notes on Chapter 23

[1] *Luke 13:26*

The Author's Conclusion

Now, Reader, I have told my dream to thee;
See if thou canst interpret it to me,
Or to thyself, or neighbor; but take heed
Of misinterpreting; for that, instead
Of doing good, will but thyself abuse:
By misinterpreting, evil ensues.
   Take heed also, that thou be not extreme
In playing with the *outside* of my dream:
Nor let my figure or similitude
Put thee into a laughter or a feud.
Leave this for *boys* and *fools*; but as for thee,
Do thou the substance of my matter see.
   Put by the curtains, look within my veil,
Turn up my metaphors, and do not fail
There, if thou seekest them, such things find
As will be helpful to an honest mind.
   What of my *dross* thou findest there, be bold
To throw away, but yet preserve the gold;
What if my gold be wrapped up in ore? —
None throws away the apple for the core.

But if thou shalt cast all away as vain,
I know not but 'twill make me dream again.